"Y   riews
w   able
tc   f the
ev   one
of   ooks
of

                                                      ithor

"   tory-
t   rvcs.
A

                                                      or of
                                                      agedy

WILD
ESCAPE

THE PRISON BREAK FROM DANNEMORA AND
THE MANHUNT THAT CAPTURED AMERICA

CHELSIA ROSE MARCIUS

DIVERSIONBOOKS

Diversion Books
A Division of Diversion Publishing Corp.
443 Park Avenue South, Suite 1008
New York, New York 10016
www.DiversionBooks.com

For more information, email info@diversionbooks.com

First Diversion Books edition February 2018.
Paperback ISBN: 978-1-63576-182-5
eBook ISBN: 978-1-63576-181-8

LSIDB/1801

"On June 3, 1845, the villagers stood in amazement as the striped black and white uniforms of the incoming draft of convicts marched from Plattsburgh to the main gate. Each had his attached ball and chain, which was also an unusual sight. The contingent of 50 men came from Mount Pleasant Prison, and to them the sight of the area must have been bewildering. Each one was probably wondering about his crime and if it was worth being sent to this forsaken spot in the Adirondacks."

—*Dannemora: Images of America*
by Rod Bigelow and Walter "Pete" Light

For Elizabeth and Rose.

FOREWORD

The first time I heard of David Sweat was the day he and Richard Matt escaped from Clinton Correctional Facility. I was immediately taken by what had occurred: two inmates had broken out of the Main (the maximum-security part of the prison), and they were the first to do it in more than a century.

As a staff reporter for the *New York Daily News* I was sent from Manhattan—about 325 miles south of the facility—to cover the escape and the three-week manhunt that followed. I spent ten days in the Adirondack region, searching for information that might advance the story. I traveled between surrounding cities, towns, and hamlets like Dannemora, Plattsburgh, Cadyville, Owls Head, Mountain View, and Malone, talking to locals. I spoke with prison guards on background about goings-on behind the barbed wire. I interviewed newly released inmates at a Mobil gas station off Route 9 in Plattsburgh—a drop-off point where these ex-cons can catch a Greyhound bus—to get a sense of what life was like on the inside both before and after the escape.

Despite their different perspectives on what had transpired, most found common ground on three major points: Matt and Sweat had outsmarted the system, they had made a mockery of the state's corrections department, and they had exposed a culture of complacency and corruption that had pervaded Clinton for years. While some worried about finding the inmates in their backyards, others were rooting for them to make it to Mexico, to Canada, or wherever they wanted to go.

They never got out of the Adirondacks.

On June 26, 2015, a U.S. Customs and Border Patrol agent killed Matt. Two days later a New York State Police sergeant captured Sweat. The media went wild with headlines. My own paper printed "Blood, Sweat & Cheers!" on its front page the following day. In the months after, reporters continued to keep tabs on the case. But, as with all breaking news, the media quickly moved on to the next big story.

I did not.

Eight months after authorities apprehended Sweat, I still wanted to know about the man who survived. By then law enforcement had a good sense of *how* Sweat and Matt did it (and a report from New York's Office of the Inspector General, released in June 2016, would provide further details regarding the execution of their plan). But there was still a single yet complicated question hanging in the air: Of all the inmates who dream of escape, what made Sweat take action and see his plan to fruition? In other words, why was *he* the one who could make it happen?

To find out, I drove to Five Points Correctional Facility in Romulus, New York, March 6, 2016—the first day in my search for the answer.

I have spent a year and a half interviewing Sweat, and I'm the only reporter he has agreed to speak with. Over the course of 20 visits, we spent nearly one hundred hours discussing the escape, his life in prison, his friendship with Matt, and the events that landed him in Clinton. In this book, I have also included passages that reveal the ugly events of his childhood and adolescence. I offer these as an explanation—*not* an excuse—as to how Sweat ended up with a life sentence behind bars.

Before I discuss the reporting, I need to say this: my relationship with Sweat has always been a professional one. Throughout this process I have been asked time and again if Sweat has been flirtatious or manipulative, or, in turn, if I have used my womanly wiles to obtain information from him. It is a shame that I have to address this subject at all, and I never intended to do so. Yet many people I talk to continue to assume that, as a female journalist, I must rely on feminine prowess in order to "get the story." Let me be clear. Sweat and I are not romantically involved, nor have either of us been inauthentic with the other for our own personal gain. I wanted to hear his story, and I believe he trusted me to tell it, to do right by it. This kind of confidence is built on a foundation of truth and respect that is earned.

Full disclosure: I was not permitted to record or take notes during my visits to Five Points—a tremendous frustration for any good journalist. After our meetings, each one about six hours long, I would go to my car (or get on the Harlem-bound overnight bus for visitors, a transportation service I later discovered) and begin to type every quote I could remember. When I had written all the quotes I could retain, I jotted notes on anything else we discussed. If he said something particularly striking (which he did quite often), I would repeat the words back to myself right after he said them, in an effort to burn the sentence into my brain. It was not an ideal method, but it proved to be much more effective than I anticipated.

Letters from Sweat were most helpful. He has written to me about his upbringing and his time on the run. One sixty-page-long account detailed what he and Matt did every day out in the woods. The dialogue I have written between him and Matt comes directly from this letter. (Unfortunately, several letters had either been lost in the mail or fell out of their envelopes during transit, as officials assigned to monitoring prison mail often opened his letters and then sent them to me without resealing. I also suspect a few were confiscated by facility personnel.) For that matter, nearly all the dialogue that appears on these pages comes directly from my interviews with the speakers, who repeated these exchanges to the best of their recollection. (There are a few instances where I have included spoken words—and, on rare occasion, a subject's internal dialogue—that do not come from direct quotes. In these instances, when paraphrasing might take the reader out of the story, I have chosen to structure the sentences as one would a quote, but without the quotation marks. An example of this is when former Clinton inmate Jeremiah Calkins listens to the radio and hears a broadcaster talking about the escape. Calkins did not recall the broadcaster or the radio station, only the essence of what the broadcaster said. I used the information he provided to write the following: *Two prisoners have escaped from Clinton,* the broadcaster said. *Their whereabouts are unknown.*) I also used the information from Sweat's writing and our conversations to construct a timeline of events from before, during, and after the escape. After comparing his notes to news and weather reports, as well as my own notes and recordings from press conferences, interviews, and additional legwork, I found that Sweat's account from memory was nearly spot on.

But this book is not only about Sweat. I have talked to corrections officers, state troopers, former inmates, contractors who work at the prison, and locals who live in the North Country. I have visited former Clinton prison seamstress Joyce Mitchell at Bedford Hills Correctional Facility, where she is serving time for aiding Matt and Sweat in the escape. I have spent hours with John Stockwell, the corrections officer who came across Matt and Sweat in his hunting cabin. I have talked with Erik Jensen, who did time at Clinton and has made prison reform his life's mission. I have spoken at length with New York State Police Sgt. Jay Cook, the man who shot and captured Sweat. And I have interviewed people from Sweat's past—his mother Pamela Sweat, his father Floyd Kenyon, and Shawn Devaul, one of the two other Binghamton boys who was with Sweat on the night that would permanently change the course of his life.

I was careful to corroborate the information from these interviews with official accounts, including the inspector general's report, as well as a number of lawsuits filed by inmates against the facility. (There were very few times that Sweat's account did not match up with the inspector general's findings. These were minor in scope, e.g. Sweat told me he smoked a stogie with Matt when their escape route was ready. The inspector general reported Sweat said he and Matt smoked a Marlboro to mark the occasion. In those instances, I went with Sweat's version of events as he relayed them to me. I have inserted footnotes to acknowledge these discrepancies.) Other important information came from the U.S. Bureau of Labor Statistics, the Department of Corrections and Community Supervision fact sheets, and information released from the office of Gov. Andrew Cuomo, the New York State Police, and the U.S. Marshal Services. I have included a full bibliography of these sources at the end of this book.

There are rare instances where one person's recollection of events differed radically from another's. This is perhaps most obvious in the case of Sweat and Joyce Mitchell. Sweat maintained that Joyce wanted to kill her husband, Lyle Mitchell; Joyce said this was never the case, and that it was Matt who talked of murdering Lyle. I have presented both of their claims in this manuscript, as there was no definitive way to decipher which narrative is true and which is false.

There were only a few people I sought out who did not want to talk to me. One of them was Corrections Officer Gene Palmer, and his part in the book is smaller because of this reticence. What I wrote about Palmer is based on interviews with inmates, contractors, and guards who know him, as well as an interview with North Country Public Radio in 2000, where he shared his sentiments about life at Clinton. I personally covered one of his court appearances, and I used my own reporting to construct that scene. For other court proceedings that I did not attend, including his arraignment and sentencing, I watched video footage and spoke to other reporters who were there. (I followed the same methods with courtroom proceedings for Mitchell and Sweat.) In addition, I revisited the interviews I conducted for the *Daily News*, including conversations with Sandy Oneill and Jeremiah Calkins.[1]

To note: the names in this work are real. The last names of Sweat's son Bradly and ex-girlfriend April (Bradly's mother) have been omitted for privacy.

The writing style of this book is influenced by that of narrative nonfiction, but it is important to mention here that I did not take liberties with the facts for the sake of good storytelling. When describing a person's thought patterns, I asked the people represented in these pages *how* they felt and *what* they were thinking during a particular moment so I could recreate those scenes and *show* what took place. If I did not obtain the necessary information to accomplish this, I did not resort to creative license. My goal was to write an accurate portrayal of the subsequent events and the people who took part in them, vetting each detail to the best of my ability.

A final note: I never went into this project with the intent of writing a book. Plain curiosity about the man I had reported on during the manhunt but had never met was the driving force behind my first visit to Five Points. Yet after I got to know Sweat, I knew this was a long-term endeavor I wanted to take on. In that way, *Wild Escape* came to me.

---

1   Sandy Oneill (or Sandra Oneill, her full name) has been misspelled in a number of publications. It should be Oneill, not O'Neill, as previously reported.

INTRODUCTION

The village of Dannemora sits on less than two square miles of remote mountain land, where a tangible isolation hangs as thick as the foothill fog. In this northeast corner of New York State, some 25 miles south of the Canadian border, temperatures dip to inhumane lows during the winter months, and summer winds can carry the crispness one might expect of an autumn breeze. Strangers seldom stop here, but for those who do, a west-bound drive along Cook Street, Dannemora's main drag, provides a glimpse of its few businesses: there's the Ford car dealership, the U.S. Post Office, the one-chair barber shop, and Liquor and Wines, its name illuminated in neon red lettering. On this stretch of Route 374, as Cook is formally known, there are traces of shuttered establishments, such as the peeling signs of Outfitters Plus Sporting Goods and Wind Chimes Country Cooking. The pubs that once dotted the thorough-fare have disappeared, though fond talk can still be heard in neighboring towns of the ol' Eight Post and Ruthie's Main Gate. A row of one- and two-story houses, most with similar screen doors and raised wooden porches, also line Cook Street; and farther west is Maggy Marketplace, the all-purpose grocer, pharmacy, and deli that sells foot-long clubs by the bundle.

To the south is St. Joseph's Catholic Church and its yard of headstones, surrounded by other simply built homes on other simply named streets, like Carter and Clark, or Maple, Orchard, and Smith. And to the north stands a thirty-foot grayish-white wall, an impressive concrete structure armed with even taller watchtowers, a fortress of sorts separating the villagers from their unlawful neighbors.[2]

Beyond this edifice lies Clinton Correctional Facility, Dannemora's stateliest citizen. For more than 170 years it has served as New York's largest all-male maximum security prison. The surrounding terrain—awesome, isolated, and rich with iron ore—proved to be the perfect place for a mid-nineteenth-century penitentiary. Built on the edge of "the Blue Line," a boundary delineating the six million acres of Adirondack Park, the untamed expanse has long served as a physical and psychological barrier to freedom for the prisoners of the cold and secluded "Little Siberia."[3]

An extended walk through its surrounding woods would wear away even the strongest of desires to flee. Thin

---

2 While there are varying figures for the height of Clinton's perimeter wall, thirty feet is the figure used by the New York Office of the Inspector General in its June 2016 report on the escape.

3 The exact origin of the nickname is unknown, but appears to date back to at least the late nineteenth century. Several historians surmise that the moniker came from the men incarcerated at Clinton during this time period.

green needles of Scotch pine can poke painfully at the skin, and thorns on the stems and leaves of the land's abundant blackberry plants can slice, swell, and infect the flesh. Thick ragweed grows high around its bogs, where sinkholes more than fifteen feet deep produce a foul scent of methane gas, and rotting lily pads leave an oily blue film on the surface of the swampy muck. No-see-ums and biting black flies flourish in the marsh, feasting off the deer, black bears, and coyotes (pronounced "ky-oats" in these parts) that also roam the wilderness. And "beaver fever"—an unpleasant bout of diarrhea, vomiting, and chills brought on by ingesting the area's untreated waters—can paralyze the most seasoned of woodsmen, who often find themselves lost under the thick canopy as the magnetism of the ore-filled land will pull the arrow of even the finest compass off course.

Such treacherous conditions left most inmates resigned to life behind the white wall, where routine had taken root for as long as anyone could remember. Dull, predictable days—beginning with 7 a.m. chow, 7:45 a.m. work, lunch at noon, and then a return to work before supper at 6 p.m.—had an unsettling effect on Clinton's guards. Rumors of COs napping on the state's time began to sift down to the village below, and whispers of other more sinister goings-on spread as far south as Saranac Lake. Locals had heard of a certain stairwell where guards struck incarcerated men with billy clubs, beating them into compliance. Others spoke of COs who, having failed to make their required rounds, had more than once found inmates strung up in their cells, feet dangling above the concrete floor, bodies already stiff.

In the days before June 6, 2015, a dangerous arrogance had seeped into Dannemora's rugged landscape, best displayed by guards who boasted that no inmate had ever escaped from the Main—the most secure building on Clinton's campus—and no inmate ever would.

PART ONE

FRIDAY, JUNE 5, 2015

CHAPTER ONE

David Sweat pushed the teeth of his last remaining bit of hacksaw blade through the inner wall of the metal steam pipe. Weeks of working from inside the dark, dank cylinder had now come down to this one final cut. Drawing his knees in, he pressed the soles of his boots against the rectangular section he had chiseled. The fiberglass lining cracked under his feet. Within minutes, that part of the channel gave way.

Spring weather had brought the kind of luck Sweat needed. Clinton had shut down its heating system for the season, and the pipe—its surface scalding during the winter months—had started to cool. By May he was able to make his first incision. Using only the hook of his hacksaw blade he carved a tiny hole into its surface.[4] He hewed away at

---

4 The State of New York Office of the Inspector General tested this method, as, according to its June 2016 report on the escape, "doubts were raised...about the possibility of cutting holes in the steam pipe with only a hacksaw blade." The Office found it was

the metal until the gap grew large enough to fit a grown man. Satisfied with the product, he crawled into the pipe, and approximately twelve feet down he began to whittle an exit. He normally would have used a drill for this work, but he could not risk the clang of power tools. Instead, he wore the metal away one inch an hour. Minutes turned to days, days turned to weeks, but Sweat did not care. He had nothing but time.

Now, tearing through some of the remaining insulation, he edged his way out of the pipe and stood fully upright in a long tunnel, which was dim and damp from years of exposure to contained steam. The underpass—used by Clinton contractors to access the piping system—was below Barker Street, a two-block residential road in Dannemora sprinkled with manholes. (Sweat did not know the street by name, but he knew that there *was* a paved road directly above the pipe.) He walked the length of the passageway, inspecting each of the exit points above his head. The first two had been chained shut, so he continued toward the end of tunnel to the last manhole, which opened with minimal effort.

Sweat peered out and saw a clearing behind the prison's powerhouse; the structure was an indication that he had gone too far. The last thing he wanted was to pop out of the ground into someone's front lawn.

He then backtracked about two hundred yards until he arrived at one of the other manholes. The plate was secured by chain, yet Sweat was able to sever a link using what blade he had left. Placing his palms flat on the sur-

---

"able to cut a three-inch-long hole in a pipe of the same material and thickness in two hours."

face, he extended his arms upward, heaving the cover onto the asphalt. He then climbed the iron ladder and lifted his head just above the lip. To the south was the powerhouse. To the north was the concrete perimeter wall.

He breathed in the free air of the Adirondacks.

"This will be perfect," he thought.

Sweat glanced at the silver watch that hung from a shoelace around his neck, its hands illuminated by a small LED light: 4:15 a.m. This was the latest he had been out since beginning work on the route—and he needed to be back on the block before the guards noticed his absence.

Even with little sleep, a sense of speed swept over him. He returned the metal cover to its proper position, sprinted down the tunnel, slid back through the steam pipe, and clambered out the other side. He then bolted toward the brick wall, removing those mortared blocks he had loosened weeks before, and scrambled through. Climbing the ladder to the catwalks, he crawled into the hole he had cut in the back wall of his cell on Clinton's Honor Block, and breathed a sigh of relief.

He checked his watch again: 4:27 a.m. Twelve minutes from start to finish, his fastest time yet.

Sweat turned to his tiny quarters. Among the towels, pillow cases, sweatshirts, and a few other miscellaneous items (a yellow Whitman's Sampler box and a Riverside Webster's II Dictionary, a paperback published in 1996 that boasted, "The Essential Reference for Successful Students") he pulled out a single Black and Mild, which he had stowed away for this very occasion.[5]

---

5   According to the New York Office of the Inspector General June 2016 report, Sweat lit a cigarette, not a cigar, as a signal to Matt

He lit the end, grabbed a small handheld mirror, and held it through the bars of his cell so that his neighbor could see his reflection.

He tapped lightly against the wall.

"Matt! Matt, get up!"

Richard Matt groaned as he rose to his feet. He peered out of his own set of bars to see Sweat's dirtied face in the looking glass. The cigar hung loosely between Sweat's lips, which, even with the smoke between his teeth, spread into a wide, satisfied grin.

"Oh my God!" Matt said. "I can't believe it! No way! I can't believe you did it!"

A celebratory stogie was part of a pact they had made during the six months of preparations. It meant the route was ready.

Sweat passed a cigar to Matt, then quickly placed a basin of water onto the hot plate in his cell. It was well past 4:30 a.m., and he needed to wash off the evidence of the overnight outing before Clinton's guards conducted standing count. As he put on a clean pair of pants and scrubbed the calluses on his palms, now toughened from the self-appointed graveyard shift, he gave Matt explicit instructions to pass on to the prison seamstress, Joyce Mitchell: she was to be in the car this evening, parked near the powerhouse, her cell phone pressed to her ear, pretending to make a call. At 12 a.m.—*exactly* 12 a.m., as he had always been a stickler for punctuality—he and Matt would emerge from the

---

that the route had been completed. In interviews with the author, Sweat said he smoked a cigar. (Specifically, a Black and Mild.) The author went with this account.

manhole near the corner of Barker and Bouck Streets by the old Dannemora school building and make for her vehicle.

Sweat scribbled the orders down on a sheet of paper and handed it to Matt to give to Joyce. The plan was clear: today would be their last behind barbed wire.

CHAPTER TWO

Fifty-five miles west of Clinton in Dickinson Center, an alarm clock rang. As Joyce Mitchell reached through the darkness to shut it off, she remembered it was Friday, the day of the week she had come to dread. She did not know yet which Friday they would carry out their plan, but she knew one thing: Matt was telling the truth when he said they were making headway on the route.

For the last six months, the fifty-one-year-old prison seamstress had dreamed of a different life from the one she was living with her husband, Lyle. Since the couple had moved into the two-story house with the rusted metal roof on Palmer Road, an extra layer of heft had settled around her waist, and the corners of her mouth had given way to gravity. Her layered, outdated 'do—its individual strands as kinked as those on the ears of a spaniel—had acquired several variations of yellow over the years, and few cosmetics had ever found a permanent place in her morning routine.

On this morning, she got dressed, brewed coffee, and packed a lunch, as always. Joyce rarely ate before leaving; it was much more pleasant to have her breakfast—today, meat and potatoes, seared and roasted the night before—while seated at her desk in Clinton's Tailor Shop 1, where she could enjoy half an hour of stillness until 8 a.m. when the inmates arrived.

In the eight years she had been employed at the facility, Joyce—whom the prisoners knew as "Tillie," her longtime nickname dating back to her high school years—had come to welcome their company. She especially liked the company of David Sweat, whom she considered the most talented worker among the men she supervised. Joyce had openly admired his proficiency with patterns and skill with a sewing machine. (He could complete thirty to forty pairs of women's prison pants within two to three days, an impressive display of dexterity.) Watching him handle each skipped stich, broken needle, or bunched-up bit of thread with his characteristic calm confidence stirred something in her she had long suppressed.

It had been nine months since Sweat was removed from her shop. His dismissal had brought on uncontrollable tears. A supervisor claimed Sweat made an inappropriate remark to another civilian employee, though Joyce suspected other motives for the decision. She knew of an anonymous note, penned by a prisoner and sent to Clinton's higher-ups, that insinuated she and Sweat were having illicit relations. Flirtations in the way of small gestures (a touch of the arm, a gentle smile) had certainly taken place between the two of them—but, as both Sweat and Joyce would later say, they had not exchanged so much as a kiss.

At that time, she saw him five days a week, seven hours a day. Now it was hardly ever, as he was no longer working under her watch.

At 6:05 a.m. Joyce opened the passenger door to the family's black Jeep Cherokee. In their one-hour commute to Clinton, she and Lyle, also an industrial training supervisor at the prison, often discussed their children, their grandchildren, and the day ahead. Today, however, Joyce shut her eyes and leaned back against the seat.

Lyle looked over. "Everything OK?" he asked.

"Yes," she said. "I just have a headache."

She had said this more than once in recent weeks. It was a convenient excuse for her staid silence.

Since Matt first told her about the plot to escape, Joyce had satisfied their every request. She had been the one to buy the hacksaw blades, chisel, drill bits, and steel punch, tools they needed to carry out the plan. (She had concealed these in a vat of raw hamburger meat to get them past the "blue shirts," as she called Clinton's guards. It had long been custom for employees to bypass bag checks and metal detector screenings. Workers frequently brought in food, which was rarely subjected to search. Hence, most of these items—even two pounds of frozen ground chuck—failed to raise eyebrows.) She had agreed to pick them up outside the prison wall, and even said she would live with them in Mexico, or wherever they ended up. The fantasy had been all-consuming: it had offered a reprieve from monotony, and a mental escape from small-town boredom. For six months the daydream had lived neat and nice in her head, where all of its dire consequences could be ignored. Now, the fear of being found out, of going even farther down this rabbit hole, filled her with unshakable panic. She knew they were almost finished with the route, and the reality of her complicity began to sink in.

As Lyle hugged the curves of the road, something told her that tonight would be the night.

CHAPTER THREE

Sweat had slimmed considerably, down nearly thirty pounds from six months of preparing their escape. It was a big drop for a fit man of five feet and ten inches who had been a solid 210 pounds, with as little body fat as a lean cut of lamb. The loss accentuated his high cheekbones, the only noticeable trace of his Blackfoot and Cherokee bloodlines. (The thirty-four-year-old appeared more Irish or English than anything else. Anglo ancestry ran on his paternal side, although the surname Sweat was taken from his mother's first husband, to whom he was not related and had never met.) His unblemished, unlined face held a certain undefinable charm; a blondish brow hung strongly over his deep-set hazel eyes, made greener against the dark leafy hue of his prison button up. A light brown goatee, at times supported by a beard, framed a pair of lips that, when parted, revealed a set of white, mostly straight teeth. These features worked particularly well together when he smiled, complementing the boyish, endearing humor for which he was known. (In his pre-Clinton life, teen girls often sought his advances, and he would entertain their interests by spraying Tommy Hilfiger cologne on his neck before performing a Keith Sweat love ballad—"no relation," he would joke.) Traces of his youth existed in the form of three black letters on three different fingers of his right hand—I on the ring, F on the middle, and B on the index—etched with Indian ink to form the acronym "IFB," which stood for "Irish-Italian Fate Brothers," a club of sorts that he and a few other boys from Binghamton had once founded. Across the upper part of his left arm the word REBEL was also inscribed, another relic from his adolescence, underscored with a line that curled on either end. (At fourteen, he had ventured out to a party with his cousin Jeffrey Nabinger[6] and Jeff's brother, Mike Benedict, who had given him the tattoos. He received two others on his arm that evening, another "IFB" and, above it, a rebel flag. These, however, have faded to only a pattern of dots that, with some imagination, resemble John Travolta in *Saturday Night Fever*.) In Clinton, he had even given a few guys body art, and was particularly proud of a sizable dragon he had drawn on the upper left shoulder and down the bicep of a fellow inmate. (A guard had seen him scoring the man's skin. The CO was about to reprimand them when, as Sweat recalled, he rolled up his shirt sleeve and said, "I'm next!")

His artistic skills had improved since meeting Matt, a

6   Sweat had long been told he and Jeffrey Nabinger were second cousins on their mother's side, though questions were later raised as to the validity of this familial connection. In any event, they considered themselves kinsman through adolescence and into adulthood.

self-proclaimed copy artist who could recreate nearly any photograph. (Matt had sketched and painted the faces of many politicians, actors, and other celebrities over the years, including Julia Roberts, Angelina Jolie, Hillary Clinton, Barack Obama, Marilyn Monroe, Oprah Winfrey, and fictional gangster Tony Soprano, which was bought by a woman on eBay for $2,000.) Matt's canvas work of a young brown and white basset hound—where each brushstroke of fur on its floppy ears held a lifelike weight and texture—had so impressed Sweat that he soon took up the craft. "Painting is about feeling and mood," he would later say. "I can start with a house. Maybe it's leaning to the left. Maybe later I want to make it go the other way. I can do that. I can mold it however I want it to look. I can escape into this place that I wish existed, the way I want the world to be. Maybe you visit a place and in that moment the light is perfect, and it's the most beautiful place you've ever seen. But then the light changes and things begin to look a little different. Painting isolates that moment. It makes it last."

Sweat first met Matt after being transferred to A-block— or the Honor Block, as it was better known. Olive-skinned with considerable girth, forty-eight-year-old Matt held a certain sway over other inmates. When he asked another prisoner for a pack of cigarettes, the inmate would get it to him free of charge. If he did not receive the respect he thought he deserved, Matt would not hesitate to shank the transgressor; when he walked down the hall, men would readily step out of his way. In Clinton he was known as "Hacksaw," the tool he used to dismember the body of his former boss, seventy-six-year-old William Rickerson, who had run a food brokerage company in North Tonawanda,

New York. Matt, then thirty-one, had roped in his strip club buddy Lee Bates to rob the businessman of cash to pay for trips to see topless women at Pure Platinum in Ontario. On December 4, 1997, they drove to Rickerson's house, knocked on his door, and demanded the dough. When Rickerson refused, Matt used a knife sharpener to beat the elderly man. He and Bates then bound Rickerson, stuffed him in a trunk, and began to drive. Every so often they pulled over and Matt would pop open the trunk to break another one of Rickerson's fingers. "Where is the money!?" he hollered again and again. "Leave the kid out of this!" Rickerson replied, referring to twenty-five-year-old Bates. "It's between you and me!" The answer enraged Matt. He pulled over once more, unlocked the trunk, and snapped the man's neck.[7]

The twenty-seven-hour trip stretched from New York to Northeast Ohio and back again. Detectives later found Rickerson's severed torso and feetless legs floating in the Niagara River. Bates, who would serve sixteen years for his part in the crime, later referred to Matt as "the Devil."

Matt's murder case greatly differed from his own, Sweat thought. Feeling a person's bones break and cutting through flesh required a more twisted mindset than pulling a trigger. He hesitated to call Matt "Hacksaw" out of a distaste for what the name represented, though using the moniker eventually became a habit. (He would later learn more disturbing details about the murder—Clinton men rarely discussed their crimes—and the new knowledge would impact how he saw his friend.) Yet Sweat still pre-

---

7   These details are based on Lee Bates's testimony at Richard Matt's murder trial in 2008.

ferred Matt to the child molesters and "homos" in prison. (He held no personal prejudice against "the gays;" he traded them goods for money because, as he put it, "Green is green.")[8] "Matt got a lot of respect," he would later say. "We had mutual respect for each other. He once said to me, 'Sweat, I'm glad I'm on your side.' I took it as a compliment. Now if you crossed him, he'd be the first to stab you. All the guys in here will be violent if they have to be, including me, and I'm not a violent person. But [when it came to me] he'd always have my back."

It was Matt who had his back after Sweat's dismissal from Tailor Shop 1. Being fired from his job meant he was removed from the third-floor, sixth-tier Honor Block cell next to Matt's and relegated to the loud, less private first floor where televised sporting events often spurred a cacophony of whoops for winning teams and whines over lost bets. But the biggest problem with Sweat's new room was how far it was from Matt's. To resolve this, Matt went to Corrections Officer Eugene Palmer (better known as Gene), an old-timer at Clinton with whom he got on well. At his bidding, Palmer asked Industrial Superintendent Scott Scholl to give Sweat another shot at industry work. Scholl agreed and assigned Sweat to Tailor Shop 8. Soon after, he was allowed to return to the cell next to Matt's. (The man who occupied Sweat's old cell had to be persuaded to move by Matt, who gave him a hundred dollars'

---

8   Sweat uses the term "homos" to describe a group of men who affiliated with one another at Clinton. Inmates in the facility are often classified according to defining traits, i.e. the Jamaicans. For Sweat, there is no intended malice behind his use of the word.

worth of cigarettes and two homemade porno books filled with voluptuous nudes.)

It was also Matt who first proposed to escape. He began to discuss the idea with Sweat in January, and Sweat—still sore about being booted from Tailor Shop 1, and fed up with prison life altogether—said he wanted in. With Sweat's cooperation, Matt's mind quickly turned to Joyce. He had seen the way she looked at his friend when they had worked together under her supervision. On the day of Sweat's dismissal, he watched her as she wept.

"What would you do if Sweat kissed you?" he later asked her. "Would you say anything?"

Joyce glanced at him over the rim of her wire frames, her yellow bangs falling behind each lens. She thought of her husband talking with a slender young blonde, a new hire at the prison who went to Lyle for guidance, which he gladly gave.

"Probably not," she said.

Matt went to back to Sweat with the news.

"She's fucking nuts. She'll bring us whatever we want, just tell me what you need and I'll get her to bring it in."

CHAPTER FOUR

By 7 a.m. Sweat had taken a seat in the mess hall. As he poured the tumbler of Raisin Bran he had purchased from the prison commissary into a bowl and filled its contents with milk—he did not like the hot cereal served there every Friday, and so brought his own—Sweat thought through their next steps. First, he'd hang his acoustic mahogany Esquire on the wall of his cell and pack the empty guitar case full of reserves he had bought the day before (thirteen pepperoni sticks, fifty-three granola bars, and a gallon bag full of peanuts, which he had emptied from individually wrapped packets, also from commissary) in addition to a few clean items of clothing (tank tops, pants, socks, underwear, one maroon sweater, and one maroon hoodie were on his packing list). There he would also fire up a large meal of salad, grilled chicken, and pizza (complete with all the available toppings) so he and Matt could load up on calories for the journey ahead. And before bed he would pan fry nine bean-filled burritos—three for him, three for Matt, and three for Joyce—as there would be few if any opportunities for pit stops before reaching Route 11, the road they would take south toward Mexico.[9]

After breakfast, Sweat was escorted to Tailor Shop 8 and took a seat next to a dark-skinned man in his early forties. In Clinton, this inmate was known as Hen, short for his nickname Hennessey, though his real name was Henry. Sweat had always appreciated the company of his work neighbor—"a good guy who did stupid things," as he liked to say. Hen had racked up a number of needless tickets for not turning off the lights when told, for staying out too late in the hall, and for gambling with other prisoners. "Those people, they don't care about you," Sweat had said to him more than once. He often imparted advice like this on inmates he took a liking to. "Be on your best behavior," he would tell them. "You want to get out and stay out. Don't come back here."

Hen was one of the few Sweat would regret never seeing again. There was no good way to say goodbye to him without giving up their plan, he thought, yet he wished to leave some sort of message the man would later understand.

"Hey, Hen," he said, leaning in. His voice lowered to a whisper. "You didn't hear this from me, but Clinton is going to be on lockdown tomorrow and I think it will be the end of my time here. Pretty sure I'm gonna get transferred. Just wanted to say it was good knowing you. Look after yourself, OK?"

---

9 Like Sweat, a number of inmates on the Honor Block had hot plates in their cells where they were permitted to cook their own meals with food they purchased at the prison commissary.

Hen turned toward him. The contours of his face creased into a knowing smile. Sweat, who only spoke when he had something important to say, had earned a certain credibility in Clinton. His words carried weight.

"You're a good man, Sweat," Hen said. "Take care of yourself."

CHAPTER FIVE

Matt had been in a good mood his entire shift—"too good of a mood," Joyce thought as she tidied up the tailor shop. For weeks he had been walking up to her desk and knocking his knuckles against it to grab her attention, and on each occasion he would whisper the same three words: "We're gettin' close." Earlier that morning he had slipped her a note, but she had not had the time nor the energy to read it. Now she had no desire to learn how close they really were.

Matt had worked with Joyce in Tailor Shop 1 since October 2013. Within one month of his assignment, he had asked her to contact his daughter Francesca in regard to some paintings he had sent her. Against Joyce's better judgment, she obliged.

That had been the extent of such requests until the following September when Sweat was removed from the shop. Immediately after the dismissal, Matt started showing Joyce more attention. It began with casual conversation about her husband, Lyle, and her children, particularly Tobey, a member of the U.S. Air Force of whom she was especially proud. Matt took note of this, and in August gave Joyce a 11-inch by 16-inch portrait of her son. A few weeks later he presented her with yet another painting, this one of her Yorkie and Boston terrier snuggling on a gray sofa. By November, she had asked him to do a portrait of her family—a gift for Lyle to commemorate their anniversary. In exchange, she brought Matt a pair of speed bag gloves, two pairs of glasses with lights on them, home-baked brownies, and other confections.

Then, in April of 2015, in some way she could not quite explain, things had taken a different turn.

"Send me a picture of you naked," he had asked her once.

"What? No! Are you crazy?"

He asked again.

"Send me a picture of you naked."

Then again.

"Send me a picture of you naked."

She had known better. She had been warned that inappropriate interactions with inmates would result in suspension, getting canned, or something much worse: incarceration. But she had also been secretly intrigued, first by Sweat, then by Matt, flattered by their interest in spite of herself.

CHAPTER SIX

Matt often accompanied Joyce to the materials room in Tailor Shop 9 where fabric and spare sewing parts were stored.[10] Nearly every day they collected supplies together, an errand that removed them from the other inmates' watchful eyes.

It was here, in a space barely large enough to fit two bodies, that she succumbed to his greatest demand.

She sunk to her wobbly knees. He loosened his pants and let them drop as he pressed his great hand on the back of her fine, feathery waves, pulling her towards him until her mouth made contact.

A month had gone by and Joyce still couldn't believe it had happened. In April, she handed him snapshots of her bare breasts, her head cropped out of the frame so that she might later deny the picture. A week or so after that he had given her a kiss, also in the materials room—the kind of kiss that can make a person forget themselves.

---

10 The "materials room" is also referred to as the "spare parts room."

Now her lips had touched a place she had never imagined they would.

"He kept me under his thumb," she had told herself. "Go against Matt and you will lose."

In the days after, Joyce composed a note to Sweat professing her love. She did not mention the encounter but supposed (wrongly, as it would turn out) that Matt had told him about that moment in the materials room.

"How could you consider sleeping with a slutbag like me?" she had written.

Her mind traveled through these recollections in the minutes before 3:15 p.m., when the prisoners in Tailor Shop 1 lined up against the wall, waiting to be chaperoned back to their cells. As Joyce gathered her belongings, a movement on the other side of the room made her glance up. She saw Matt's arm cocked in the shape of an L, his fist in the air. He looked right at her and grinned.

She had not yet read Sweat's final note, the one Matt had slipped to her that morning with a list of instructions on where to wait for them. Now, as he stood there with his hand raised, she knew this was the signal he had once spoken of—the gesture he said he would give to let her know that this night was the night they would escape.[11]

Her head, still throbbing from that morning, felt uncomfortably light.

---

11 In her voluntary written statement to the New York State Police taken June 7, 2015, Joyce told investigators, "He [Matt] told me that they were getting out tonight and we were all going to be together, me, him and inmate Sweat…and we were all going to leave together." Joyce provided a different narrative during subsequent interviews with the author, which included Matt's hand gesture and Sweat's letter with instructions. Sweat later confirmed the existence of this letter.

CHAPTER SEVEN

Months back, Sweat considered simply climbing over the prison's perimeter wall. He heard the middle watchtower along Cook Street had been unmanned for some time, years even (it was condemned due to its crumbling staircase, several Clinton contractors later said), but he first needed to get out of his cell. Upon inspecting its lock, he thought he might be able to detach the door by removing its screws. Using a lump of putty, he made an impression of the Torx screw head, its silhouette resembling a six-point star. Once the clay-like substance had hardened, he brushed its surface with a dab of paint. When it was firm, he pressed the putty onto a scrap of paper as one would a rubber stamp, its imprint a reference for the size and shape of tool he needed. He handed the note to Matt, who passed it on to Joyce in Tailor Shop 1. She purchased the bits from a store in Malone and brought them back to Matt, who tucked all three in a pair of headphones and snuck them to Sweat during recreational hours on the Honor Block's first-floor flats.[12]

This note became the first in a string of written interactions with Joyce that evolved from practical instructions to something more. Along with lists regarding what tools he would need, Sweat began to paint a stirring image of a life where they would make love on the beach, and live in a bungalow that he would build. Joyce responded to each of these notes (or "kites," as Sweat calls them) with the same flirtatious adoration. The notion of a younger, fine-looking man being interested in her offered a faint promise of lifting the tedium that had clouded most of her existence.

Sweat eventually scrapped the idea to detach the door. Even if he removed the hinges, Matt would never make it. He had been much more fit when he scaled a perimeter fence at Erie County Correctional Facility years before, part of a string of failed jailbreaks in his life of incarceration. (He had been unsuccessful in other attempts to escape—the second from a prison in Mexico where he did time for fatally stabbing a strip club patron in the border city of Matamoros, and the third from Niagara County Jail during his 2008 trial for Rickerson's murder.[13])

Matt joked about a few other schemes ("Let's build

---

12 Upon leaving the tailor shops, inmates rarely passed through a metal detector. On those occasions that they were asked to pass through this device, electronics were typically not scanned. These practices were in breach of protocol.

13 Matt had told Sweat he had been in the facility where famed escapee Joaquin "El Chapo" Guzman had been held, though it was unclear if he meant Puente Grande or Altiplano Federal Penitentiary, as the drug kingpin had done time in both.

a hang glider and fly over the wall!" he suggested, only half-kidding) before coming up with an idea that Sweat could work with.

"We'll get in the sewer, something like that."

"Something like that," Sweat thought. He felt sure that if he could cut through the steel wall in the rear of his cell, he would be able to access the catwalk, a narrow open bridge that extended between the various housing blocks. If he could find a way to the prison's underground tunnels, he knew he could find a way out.

CHAPTER EIGHT

By mid-February, Sweat and Matt began to put their plan in motion. Neither uttered a word about it to anyone. (In recent months, one inmate had talked loosely to Sweat about breaking out of Clinton. "How many people have you told about this?" Sweat had asked. The man started rattling off names before Sweat stopped him. "Don't tell me anything else. I don't want to know anything about it." Within weeks of their conversation, Sweat heard the prison had found out about the inmate's plan.) Sweat also ended all communication with his mother and his girlfriend of five years, the sister of a prisoner named Frank who had once seen a photo of him in a tank top and asked her brother to introduce them. Writing letters would open them up to questioning by investigators, he thought. He hoped he would spare them the trouble of what was surely to come.

Through Matt, Sweat asked Joyce to smuggle in two sets of hacksaw blades. She stowed the first set in the side pocket of her lunch bag, and the second in the raw frozen hamburger meat—the same method she used to transport the two chisels, two drill bits, and steel punch. Joyce delivered each of these items to Matt who, upon receiving them, taped the tools to his bare chest. At the end of his shift, he simply walked back to his cell with Palmer—who frequently failed to perform mandatory frisks—being none the wiser.

They used these tools to begin slicing holes along the air vents in the back of their adjacent cells. Sweat concealed the cut lines with clear packing tape and interior paint, given to the prisoners to spruce up their assigned rooms. (By coloring the adhesive in the same mint green hue—and by also placing strips of painted tape on other random parts of the wall to create a uniform look—he successfully masked the hole.) They worked during their allotted ninety minutes of evening recreation, when racket from inmates playing blackjack and dominoes on the first-floor flats drowned out the sounds of the blades gnawing at steel. While one of them toiled away, the other held a mirror between the bars to keep a lookout for anyone coming down the company.[14] Both had long established a routine of creating portraits and landscapes throughout this hour and a half of leisure, and with the assumption that they were painting, few guards ever checked on them. When they finished for the evening, each pushed his bed back against the rear wall, the legs of which were padded with cloth so that the metal frames slid across the floor in silence. (During the day, Sweat kept his favorite work of

---

14 "Company" is a section of the Honor Block. There are six companies on the Honor Block. Sweat and Matt's cells were a part of "6 Company."

art, "Midnight in the Park," propped up against the hole for good measure.)

Within four weeks, both had successfully cut out the air vents, leaving a rectangular entry to the catwalks. Upon completion, Sweat began exploring the bowels of Clinton. (Of the two men, he had the more mathematical mind, which, as it turned out, was perfect for such a task. This had been fine with Matt, whose size and claustrophobia would have made him more of a burden than an asset.) Moving underground from A-Block to B-Block proved easy at first, but as he made his way from B-Block to C-Block he encountered a wall. A bundle of pipes ran through an opening toward the top of this barrier, with a space just wide enough for him to wiggle through. Yet from eyeballing it, Sweat saw this area would not accommodate Matt's oversized midsection, and so he spent two nights enlarging the gap. Once through this hole, he hit yet another wall between C-Block and the industry building, this one made of bricks. Each night he chipped away at bits of mortar until he could remove enough brick to widen the opening. An 8-pound sledgehammer Sweat found in an unsecured gang box left by one of Clinton's contractors accelerated the process. Sweat timed his blows to the bricks with the clanging of the old, warped pipes, and by late April, he had completed the entryway.

The prison's perimeter wall, its base firmly planted underneath the facility, presented another temporary dilemma. The only way out of the tunnels below Clinton was through the wall, and the only way through the wall—too thick to breach, as he had previously attempted to do with a sledgehammer and sharpened bolt—was through the blistering steam pipe that passed through the concrete edifice.

Sweat would soon have unexpected luck: Clinton shut off its heat in May, and the pipe cooled enough for him to begin cutting his way through.

• • •

At 3:15 p.m., Sweat packed his sewing tools for the last time. As he lined up with the group of inmates waiting to be escorted back to their cells, he saw Joyce standing with the other civilians preparing to punch out. He saw her only once a day now, always at this hour.

Sweat glanced in her direction. He pressed the silver cross she had given him between his thumb and forefinger.[15] Joyce looked up at him and took hold of her own necklace—yet something in her expression gave Sweat pause. There was a slight contortion in her face—perhaps a raise of the brow, a widening of the eyes, a flexion of the neck causing the muscles to tense—that made him feel something was off.

A moment later he was whisked away with the other prisoners. As he headed back to the Honor Block, something in him said that this would be the last time he saw the seamstress.

---

15 After Sweat had been removed from Tailor Shop 1, Joyce had ordered a two hundred dollar necklace from a catalogue of facility-approved items. She had given the pendant and chain to Matt to give to Sweat, but Matt had kept the chain. He told Sweat it did not look like real silver, yet Sweat believed he decided to sell it and pocket the cash.

CHAPTER NINE

At 11 p.m. Corrections Officer Ronald Blair conducted the day's final standing count. As Blair walked down the company checking that each cell had a body, a deep sense of satisfaction washed over Sweat. He had always felt Blair was unreasonably disruptive during his count duties, sticking a flashlight between the bars of cells to bang on the feet of sleeping inmates. Sweat had kept track of the guard's work schedule so that they would make sure to sneak out during his shift. To Sweat, breaking out on Blair's watch would be extra sweet.

Having determined that all the inmates were present, the CO resumed his position at the other end of the hall. The lights in the cells went out.

Matt and Sweat let a minute pass before they changed out of their prison uniforms. Sweat collected the remainder of his supplies, including his handheld radio and the photocopied pages of a 2015 Rand McNally Road Atlas from

Joyce. Before leaving, Matt pulled a black skull cap over his head and went to writing two notes—the first, "Time to Go Kid! 6-5-15," he scrawled on his wall calendar, illustrating it with images of his own artwork; the second he scribbled on a pad of paper placed on his table: "You left me no choice but to grow old & die in here. I had to do something."

They looked around one last time, then ducked out of the holes where the air vents had been and stepped down the ladder onto the catwalks. The men moved quickly through Clinton's snaking underbelly until they reached the first wall. Sweat removed the bricks he had previously loosened so that they could crawl through. After reaching the other side, he replaced the bricks again.

A few more steps led them straight to the steam pipe. Matt gave Sweat a sideways look.

"We're going in there?" he said, surveying the eighteen-inch diameter tube with great suspicion.

"Yep," Sweat said, smiling. "I'll go first. Come in right after me."

He climbed in and scooted until he reached the exit hole, with Matt close behind. As he pushed himself upright, Matt's voice echoed from inside the pipe.

"HELP! I'm stuck!"

Sweat squatted to see Matt's cap had slid off and landed in the small space between the pipe and his ample gut. Sweat rummaged through his pack and got out a bedsheet, twisting it like a rope and tossing it down.

"Grab hold of this!" he called out.

Matt grasped the fabric and Sweat yanked. When he

had Matt close enough, Sweat lifted him from under the armpits and pulled.

As he did so, Matt's pants caught on the lip of the opening.

"Aw, Hacksaw!" Sweat said with a grin as he saw the crack of his friend's backside. "You shouldn't have!"

Once upright, the two walked through the tunnel to the manhole under the corner of Barker and Bouck Streets. After ten minutes, Sweat checked his watch: 11:45 p.m.

He threw off his thick sweater and the cloth wrapped around his head, climbed up the ladder, and unhooked the chain he had severed the night before.

"Maybe she'll be here early," he said, shoving the metal plate over as he raised his head through the manhole.

To the north he could make out grayish white wall. To the south was the outline of the powerhouse.

He saw no sign of the black Jeep Cherokee.

Sweat lowered himself back into the tunnel and turned to Matt.

"What if she doesn't show?" he asked.

Matt shook his head. "She'll show."

Sweat paused before responding.

"Well if she don't, we've got two choices: go on foot or go back and wait 'til Monday."

Matt looked like he would rather eat dung.

"I'm not going back through that pipe!"

Sweat nodded.

"OK. Exactly at twelve we go."

Fifteen minutes passed. Sweat stuck his head out again. He looked out toward Smith Street for a moment before lowering himself once more.

"She's not there," he said.

Matt's mouth hung open. He had banked on her coming. He would've bet on it. He never thought she would bail.

"Come on, it's too late for that," Sweat said. Wondering where she was would only waste time they did not have, he thought. "Let's go."

Yet as soon as they heaved themselves out of the manhole, a pair of headlights appeared down the road.

Matt took off. Sweat tore after him, his guitar bag bouncing awkwardly on his back.

Just then, a figure in the distance called out.

"Hey, what are you fucking scumbags doing in my yard!?" someone yelled.

Sweat slowed his gait.

"Sorry bro, we're on the wrong street!" he called out. "He was just trying to cut through!"[16]

The man, seemingly content with the answer, disappeared into the dark.

There was no time to consider the exchange. Sweat was focused on one thing: getting them far away from Clinton.

He caught up with Matt—which was fairly easy, as Matt's clunky old boots sunk into the soaked lawn with each step—and jerked him back by the shirt.

"Don't take off like that!" he said. Running made them look like fugitives.

They scanned Smith Street again, walking past the powerhouse to check one last time for Joyce.

Sweat had always liked the seamstress. He considered

---

16 The inspector general's report quotes Sweat differently. The author opted to go with how Sweat put it to her.

her "a nice person," at least until recently, when in one of her notes she referred to Lyle as "the glitch" in their plan. To Sweat, Joyce had expressed in so many words that her husband needed to be dealt with accordingly. Matt had spent some time thinking about what they were going to do with Joyce once she joined them. His schemes were malevolent (one idea had been to tie her up to a tree in Virginia and leave her with her cell phone and a letter to her husband Lyle from them, explaining that she said she wanted to kill him; another had been to take her to the house in Dickinson, reveal her intentions to Lyle, and then tie them both up to chairs), but murdering Lyle had never entered the equation. From the moment she first mentioned "the glitch," Sweat said he had lost all respect for her. The events of the evening reaffirmed his feelings.

They made their way southwest to the corner of Emmons, near St. Joseph's Catholic Church, passing the old Delaware and Hudson Railway, the ties of which had since been torn up, although the path was still used by skidoos.[17] They veered back north towards Cook. "Better to stick to the main roads 'til dawn," he thought. He knew that, come morning, troopers would be tracking every footpath in the vicinity of Dannemora.

Matt pulled out his Army-style coat, as the cool air had brought on a sudden chill. For more than eight miles they kept to the county route as it circled around Chazy Lake, nestled at the center of a triangle formed by Lyon, Johnson, and Ellenburg Mountains. With Sweat's guitar case and

---

17 "Skidoo" is a colloquial term for a snowmobile. The word is used in upstate New York and Canada. It comes from the brand, "Ski-Doo," which manufactures snowmobiles.

Matt's military jacket, they might have mistaken the men for two musicians walking home from a late-night gig.

After some time, Matt spoke again.

"She should have come with us," he said. "They're going to get her for this."

CHAPTER TEN

Two miles from the manhole, Joyce sat in the emergency room of Alice Hyde Medical Center in Malone, admitted for a panic attack.

Earlier that day, at around 3:20 p.m., Joyce had met Lyle at the Jeep in Clinton's parking lot. He suggested going out for dinner. She agreed to it and, without speaking, lay her head back as Lyle drove to Malone's No. 1 Chinese Restaurant. Joyce selected two egg rolls, a handful of noodles, and a few slices of chicken from the buffet but barely touched the plate. Back home, she retreated to her recliner and shut her eyes. A weight seemed to sit squarely on her sternum, making her feel short of breath. Lyle wanted to take her to the emergency room but she said no, a nap would surely take care of it.

It didn't.

By around 9 p.m. she and Lyle were in the ER waiting to be seen. The pressure in her chest mounted as the hands of the clock on the wall ticked: 10 p.m., 10:30 p.m., 11 p.m., 11:30 p.m.

Then, midnight.

Invisible fingers clutched the hollow cavity around her heart, filling her soul with renewed fear. Matt and Sweat were out, and they knew she was not there. The terror that now took hold was as much a fear *of* them as it was a fear *for* them, intertwined with a fear for herself and for what was to come.

•   •   •

Something on the Honor Block seemed amiss to Corrections Officer Ronald Blair. While the gallery lights on the company had been flipped on for the mandatory morning standing count (and, in response, the other inmates had turned on the lights in their quarters), cells A6-22 and A6-23 on the third floor appeared to be dark.

Blair strode over to 22 first, yelling for Matt to get his ass out of bed. The inmate, however, did not move. Thoroughly annoyed, Blair reached through the bars and shook the metal bed frame. Still, nothing.

Fuming, he went into the cell, pulled back the sheets, and nearly puked. A makeshift dummy was in the place where Richard Matt should have been. Blair lunged towards Sweat's cell, unlocked the door, and threw off the covers to find a rudimental dummy comprised of a red hooded sweatshirt and a stuffed pair of brown pants.

Blair cried out and made for the staircase, stumbling down the steps as he went.

PART TWO

DAY ONE

SATURDAY, JUNE 6TH

Lou Ann Nielson woke up just after the sun rose. She pulled on her scrubs and poured herself a mug of coffee and a tall glass of orange juice as she did every Saturday before an eight-hour shift at Champlain Valley Physicians Hospital. For thirty-five years, Lou had watched distressing changes along Route 374—the closure of its dollar theater, the shutdown of Pearl's Department Store, the end of the neighborhood pub, Billy's in the Middle. The village had become increasingly depressed, a forgotten place between Potsdam and Plattsburgh.

The one thing that hadn't changed was the presence of the prison, which she saw every morning on her way out. Yet with time the facility had blended into the backdrop, so much so that she gave it little thought.

At 6:15 a.m., toting a packed lunch of leftover steak, salad, and sweet potatoes, fifty-five-year-old Nielson walked out of the two-story yellow house and made her way toward her four-door blue Honda Highlander parked along Barker Street. She climbed into the car, turned on the ignition, and pressed the gas pedal. Not thirty feet later her tires took a familiar dip over the metal edge of the closest manhole, rendering a brief clink as they went.

It had been a typical morning at the hospital's emergency department with its routine bumps, bruises, and broken bones, until break time when another nurse ran toward her, waving a cell phone in the air.

"Lou!" she said. "Get on Facebook! See what's going on in Dannemora!"

"What in the world," Lou thought to herself. She grabbed her own phone and went through her news feed, poring over her friends' most recent posts.

She did not have to scroll far before coming across two faces she had never seen before: the first, an olive-skinned man with slicked back hair, thick brows, and a cleft chin covered by graying scruff; the other, a thinner, lighter-skinned man with a blondish-brown goatee and slightly crooked nose.

She turned to her colleague.

"Oh, man. This is not good."

Nielson pulled up a number for her housemate, Phil Maynard. If there was anyone she wanted to talk to at a moment like this, it was him.

He answered her call after one ring.

"What's going on?" she said before he could speak. "I seen this on Facebook, something about two inmates escaping from Clinton. Is it true?"

"I'll talk to you later," Maynard said. "B.C.I. is here."

With that, he hung up.

Nielson had lived with the retired CO long enough to know he was referring to the Bureau of Criminal Investigation, a plainclothes detective branch of the New York State Police that assisted local and county law enforcement agencies with special investigations.

"If B.C.I. has been brought in," she thought, "it must be big."

• • •

"We need a car."

Matt had repeated this assertion half a dozen times since leaving the manhole. The excitement of his newfound freedom had quickly been replaced by rattled nerves. This was not the case with Sweat, who for the last six months had experienced a daily sense of autonomy he had not felt since first being locked up. For Matt, this sovereignty had not quite sunk in, and the effect was unsettling.

Still, Sweat understood Matt's concern. The plan had never been to walk this far, and a large, irritating, liquid-filled blister had begun to swell on his left heel. (They already had to stop once to switch into a pair of clean, dry socks, which helped ease the sore and stave off infection.) But stealing a vehicle was out of the question. Finding a car would most likely require breaking into a house to retrieve the keys, and Sweat was not looking to commit a home invasion less than twelve hours after their escape. They had also agreed to take every precaution possible so no one got hurt. Forceful entry would certainly end in injury, or something much worse. Besides, Sweat thought, newer cars with their computer chips and GPS capabilities would be easier for law enforcement to track. If they were to swipe one, it would have to be old—but even then, it would only be a matter of time before someone reported a vehicle missing. It had taken them six months to get this far. He was not about to risk getting caught now.

The men were heading for Route 11. The nearly 320-mile stretch was north of Dannemora but traveled west through the towns of Chateaugay and Malone before veering south, bisecting Pulaski and Syracuse. This highway fed into larger, southbound interstates they might be able to take to Mexico—a plan that was still in the cards even though Joyce had bailed. Sweat had considered traveling north, but that might play them into the hands of law enforcement. He guessed the Stateys (as he called the troopers) would think they were going straight for the Canadian border. Moving west, he hoped, would throw them off.

A street sign indicated they were about one mile north of Saranac. "Too far south," Sweat thought as he scarfed down a Milky Way and redirected them once more. Later, another sign with the words "New Land Trust"—a 287-acre oasis for birdwatchers and cross-country skiers at the foot of Lyon Mountain—suggested they were back on the right path.

They had put several miles between them and the prison by the time they reached a three-way junction in the road. At the corner stood a white house where a little girl's bike had been propped up against a tree in the front yard. (Matt half-joked about swiping the set of wheels, to which Sweat emphatically said no.)

The men continued west, smoking Marlboro Reds as they walked.

"Man, my feet are fucking killing me," Matt called ahead. He was already several paces behind.

"C'mon," said Sweat. Stopping would make it harder to start up again, he thought. They needed to take advantage of the clear night before inevitable summer showers would muddy their path and slow their progress. The COs would soon realize they were not in their cells. It would only be a matter of time before a manhunt was underway. "We'll rest soon enough."

They had hiked at least ten miles by dawn (the exact distance, with all its turns and twists, was impossible to track) when an unexpected sound from the side of the road sent a small jolt through Sweat's spine. He swore he could feel a pair of eyes on them, staring through the darkness. A faint rustle had come from somewhere in the brush, from some place he could not quite see.

Sweat turned his body slightly toward the leaves before he saw it: a large black bear feeling its way through the wilderness. Sweat smiled. He had not been this close to nature in thirteen years.

He did not mention the bear to Matt until they were well past the place where he had seen the animal. And it was good thing he hadn't; Matt was one beat away from a heart attack when he heard about the close encounter. Later, another swish from the bushes caused him to jump with a start. Sweat laughed, pointing toward the source of the sound—a brown deer, which readily leapt back into the woods.

Farther along, they found a place to rest. Sweat sat on the ground, his legs crossed, and pulled out his second Milky Way of the night. He split the chocolate-covered candy bar with Matt, and they munched away for a minute or so before reluctantly resuming their walk. As the sun rose both agreed it was time to move off the main road. They knew that by now Clinton's guards would surely have noticed their absence, and the state troopers would soon be out searching.

After a few more miles, Matt needed to stop again. He pulled off the path, and removed his socks and boots.

"I don't even want to look at mine!" said Sweat, watching as Matt tended to his chafing skin. His feet had grown red and raw from traipsing in the worn-out leather.

As Matt rested, Sweat scanned the surrounding terrain until his eyes fell on a raised barrier in the land. They could not see the other side of this berm from where they sat, which worried him; someone could be hiding behind it and he and Matt would be none the wiser. He walked over to inspect the embankment and looked back toward Matt. From the point where he now stood, Sweat could clearly see him.

He headed back toward his friend.

"We cannot stay here," he said. "We have to move away to avoid being seen."

Matt grumbled at the prospect of moving but nodded, hoisting himself up.

Through the woods they went, until they came across a poster-size map tacked to a wooden board. After a quick study of its key and color-coded paths, he could see that they had ventured slightly off course. Reorienting himself, he selected Trail Number 9—dubbed the Guadeloupe Trail—which would lead them west once more.

By 8 a.m. fatigue had finally set in. The men gathered all the fallen branches they could find to build a lean-to, hoping the simple structure would provide some protection from prying eyes.

As they set up camp, Sweat emptied his one-gallon ziplock bag of its soaps, toothpaste, razors, and fresh underclothes; this bag, he thought, would be perfect for collecting fresh water from the nearby brook.

After filling the ziplock, he returned to the site. Burning the end of a fingernail clipper with a lighter, Sweat began to pop the blisters that had not yet erupted. He and Matt had come to the conclusion that the Dr. Scholl's gel inserts they had slipped into their shoes the night before were, as Sweat put it, "complete shit."

"You hungry?" Sweat asked. He needed to talk his mind off the sores.

"Yeah, what do you have?"

Sweat brought out the burritos he had fried up the night before. Matt's eyes widened before he broke into a hearty laugh.

"Who brings burritos on a prison break!?"

Sweat grinned. "I do." He had let each ingredient—black beans and cheddar cheese, hot sauce, and caramelized onions—sizzle in its own oil-slicked pan over the hot plate in his cell, ensuring that every component had cooked to perfection.

Matt grabbed one and dug in.

"Man," he said, his mouth stuffed with flour tortilla. "These are some good breakout burritos!"

Sweat shook his head.

"No, they're prison break burritos. Breakout burritos just sounds like you want to, well, break out some burritos!"

And so they laughed and ate and wondered aloud just how bad things were back at Clinton.

• • •

Jeremiah Calkins woke up early for his morning shift in the mess hall of Clinton's Annex, the building adjacent to the Main, the latter of which housed the Honor Block. Not wanting to be late for work, the twenty-eight-year-old, a slight white man from Salamanca, waited quietly in his cell for a CO to escort him to the mess.

No one ever came. And when a guard did eventually walk by, he told Calkins to stay put.

Confused, the inmate decided to listen to his handheld radio purchased from the commissary and wait for further instruction. Calkins flipped on the device and tuned in to the local news.

A voice came over the frequency.

Two prisoners have escaped from Clinton, the broadcaster said. *Their whereabouts are unknown.*

He froze.

"Impossible," he thought. "No one could do that. Not from here. Not from Clinton."

• • •

The summer light streamed in through the windows of the Honor Block as Gov. Andrew Cuomo strode along the sixth tier's narrow walkway, peering into the unlit cells on his right as he made his way down the company.

He stopped in front of A6-22 and A6-23.

"That's solid," he said with a sniff, giving a glance at the steel bars that ran six stories down to the ground floor. The governor grimaced as he turned toward a prisoner in one of the compartments next to Matt's now vacant mint-green room, its width no more than a tall man's wingspan. "They must have kept you awake with all that cuttin', huh?"

Cuomo had planned on attending the 147th Belmont Stakes that Saturday to watch thoroughbreds race in the last leg of the Triple Crown. That plan had changed before he ever left his home in Mount Kisco, New York. At around 7 a.m. he received word of the prison break at Clinton Correctional Facility. The state police had flown him out of Westchester County Airport to Albany and then on to Plattsburgh, before driving him 15 miles west to Dannemora.

By the early afternoon he was on a guided tour of the escape route, ascending the catwalks behind the Honor Block and examining the rectangular holes cut in the back of the two sixth-tier cells. Shedding his blue sport coat, Cuomo descended the rusty thin ladder that led to the underground tunnels. He inspected the brick wall where the mortar had been chiseled away. He shined an orange flashlight into the steam pipe, toward the opening that had been carved into its fiberglass surface. As he bent down to have a better look, the governor saw a yellow square note tacked to the pipe with a tiny round magnet. A perfect black circle formed a sort of smiley-face, complete with two slanted eyes and two bucked teeth, the crown of its head topped with a triangular hat. Below its chin, four words had been printed in neat, flowery penmanship: "Have A Nice Day!"

• • •

"Heads up!"

The words came from someone in the gaggle of reporters, assembled in front of Clinton, who spotted the governor walking their way. By mid-day, the village had seen a startling level of media activity. Almost every major daily and cable news network was staked outside the prison. Scribblers from the *Times Union* and *Press-Republican*, pens and notepads stuffed in purses and back pockets, had also descended upon Dannemora. Television trucks pulled up and parked along the thin grassy strip between Cook Street and Clinton's concrete wall near the facility's Training Center, a stone building several hundred paces from the Main. The cameramen set up their tripods (or "sticks" as media people call them) and clipped their mics to a lectern, which bore the blue and gold New York State seal. Nearby were three poster-sized images on three large easels: the first, a black and white aerial shot of the facility; the others prison-issued identification photos of two men, one with scruff surrounding his heavy cleft chin, the other younger, with green eyes and a blondish-brown goatee.

The journalists huddled to hear Cuomo, who now took his place in front of the crowd. Beside him was Anthony J. Annucci, head of the New York State Department of Corrections and Community Supervision (DOCCS), a thick-mustached man wearing a windbreaker bearing the word COMMISSIONER in gold lettering.

Annucci began with a rundown of the facts—David Sweat, born June 1980, height five feet eleven inches, weight 165 pounds, and Richard Matt, born June 1966, height six feet, weight 210 pounds—had escaped from Clinton. Both were serving time for murder: Matt twenty-five years to life, and Sweat life without parole.

"This morning we noticed during the standing count at 5:30 a.m. at this facility the two cells which were joining each other were empty," Annucci said. "The search revealed that there was a hole cut out in the back of the cell [from] which these inmates escaped…This was a very elaborate plan, but we are only at the very preliminary stages of determining exactly what happened. Security is our utmost priority—keeping the inmates safe, keeping staff safe, and keeping all of the general public safe."

Major Charles E. Guess of the New York State Police spoke next.

Two hundred law enforcement officers had already begun the search, he said, ticking off the various agencies that had sent personnel to the area: the state police, DOCCS, the FBI, the New York State Forest Rangers, the U.S. Marshals Service, and the sheriff's departments from both Clinton and Franklin Counties. SWAT units had been deployed. Three choppers, two from the state police and a third from the U.S. Department of Homeland Security, had been circling the area for hours. Dogs had been brought in to track the scent.

"No stone is being left unturned," he said.

Then, Cuomo faced the media.

"This is a first time in this institution's history that anyone has escaped from the maximum portion—maximum-security portion of this facility [sic]. The facility opened in 1865 so this is quite an unusual occurrence. As you heard from the commissioner, it was an elaborate plot. We went back and pieced together what they did. It was elaborate, it was sophisticated, it encompassed drilling through steel walls and steel pipes, so this was not easily accomplished…

"First order of business is to find the two individuals and return them to prison. And we're working on that and we're asking for the help of the people across the state today. These are two dangerous individuals.

"There's no doubt it was an extraordinary act. You look at the precision of the operation, it was truly extraordinary and unusual and almost impossible to duplicate…We want to find out exactly what happened and one of the big questions is, where did the tools come from?"

• • •

Tech. Sgt. Jay Cook arrived at Highland Greens Golf Course in Brushton, New York, early Saturday morning. He rarely played the game, six to seven times a year at best, but he had agreed to participate in a benefit tournament with three of his buddies from Troop B of the New York State Police.

As he warmed up his swing, Cook noticed that they were missing one of their men.

"Hey, where's Kurt Taylor?"

"Oh, Kurt's not coming," said Joe Tatro, who worked out of the Malone barracks with Cook. "There's been an escape."

Taylor, a senior investigator in the troop, had phoned to say that he had been unexpectedly pulled into work for a prison break.

Cook had never heard of a single inmate, let alone two,

making it out of Dannemora alive. He was born and raised in the North Country. He knew what lay ahead for the men fresh out of Little Siberia.

"Well, they'll find them," he said. "They won't get far."

• • •

The thumping of chopper blades sounded overhead.

"A Huey," Sweat thought.

They could not see the Bell UH-1 Iroquois searching through the dense foliage of the Adirondacks. Both stopped to listen, looking at one another, then up into the patches of sky visible through the canopy of green. The helicopter's rotary wings produced a steady staccato thud as they whipped the air, the thrust of each blade drawing it closer to where they stood.

For a moment, the hum faded. Then, like a boomerang, the faint whirring grew louder again.

Sweat turned to Matt.

"It's running a pattern. We're just outside of it but way too close if we can hear it. We can't stay here."

He guided them west over a narrow stream. As they trudged, the ground began to rise, forcing their bodies to fold forward to balance the weight on their backs. Matt took his flashlight out to illuminate the way. The landscape, littered with leaves and rotting limbs, became more barren with each step. Sweat's eyes roved upwards. He scanned the sky until his gaze fell on the North Star, their glittering guide through the dark.

• • •

BINGHAMTON, NEW YORK—1985

That year, the Sweats moved from Deposit, New York, to 99 Robinson Street on the east side of Binghamton, New York, where, apart from a two-pump gas station and Cortese Restaurant—a pizza place serving thin-crust pies—not much else existed. The city had once been called the "Valley of Opportunity," though it was hard to believe that now. Binghamton had been the anchor of the region's Triple Cities, manufacturing hubs that included Johnson City and Endicott in the state's Southern Tier. Near the turn of the twentieth century it was the second-largest producer of cigars in the United States. Within three decades, shoes also topped its list of homegrown wares. Technology too had once found its place in the valley; it was there that the innovator Edward Link had constructed the world's first flight simulator, and International Business Machines, now known as IBM, was previously based. Such development had brought about the construction of several railroad lines, connecting Binghamton's booming factories to other parts of the country.

David, the youngest of the Sweat brood, had taken to walking these tracks alone. The rails of the New York, Susquehanna & Western Railway (the "Susie-Q" as it was called) practically ran through the backyard of their new house—or rather, the house where his family now lived, which was still new to him. The low rent had appealed to his mother Pamela, a single parent who considered the place suitable enough for her three children and jumped at the opportunity.

But David preferred to stay away from the house altogether. During his daily wanderings, circling the large heaps of ore piled along the railway, he thought back to Deposit, the rural town about forty miles southeast where they had last lived. There he had friends like Ronnie—with whom he had once spent several days on a farm chasing sheep to shear—and crazy, lovable relatives like Uncle James Tuttle, his mother's brother whom he held in high regard. (It was Jimmy who, during David's first target practice, held a .30-06 Springfield Bolt-Action Rifle so his nephew could squint through its scope and home in on a cracked milk jug dangling from a branch by its handle. "I want to shoot that jug outta' that tree!" David had cried to the small group of amused spectators. "Take your time. Aim carefully," Jimmy had told him. David dialed in and gently squeezed the trigger. The bullet sent shards of glass into the air.)

Had they stayed in Deposit, he thought, his life might have been normal.

DAY TWO

SUNDAY, JUNE 7TH

After the opening of Auburn Prison in 1816 and Sing Sing in 1826, New York was in need of another penitentiary.[18] The state legislature believed a facility in the Adirondacks would be ideal for two main reasons: the fresh foothill air would be good for a growing number of inmates infected by tuberculosis, and convicts could also be used as labor to mine and manufacture the region's bounty of iron ore. The workshops of Auburn and the marble quarries of Sing Sing—where revenue from inmate labor offset operational costs—thus provided a blueprint for another self-sufficient institution. The legislature gave its blessing May 13, 1844, for the construction of what was to be called Clinton

---

18 Auburn Prison, now Auburn Correctional Facility, is also (less frequently) referred to as Auburn State Prison. Sing Sing Prison, commonly referred to as simply "Sing Sing," was later renamed Sing Sing Correctional Facility. Records of the official dates of opening vary. Sing Sing is considered to have opened in 1826, though it would be two more years before construction was completed.

Prison.[19] Within sixteen months the facility took in its first tenants—fifty men out of Plattsburgh who quickly went to work mining the minerals from nearby Lyon Mountain.[20] In 1893, that number grew to 1,000. By June 5, 2015, a total of 2,653 inmates—1,917 in the Main and 736 in the Annex, the lower security part of the prison—would call Clinton home.

In its early years, nearly every man in Dannemora worked at the facility. Hotels, houses, and boutiques were soon built to accommodate a growing civilian population. Paved streets replaced plank roads. New railways allowed for passenger trains to roll through town. Other buildings, including a factory, hospital, and bath house, were built by convicts on Clinton's grounds. The Warden's Residence—a stately Victorian manor on Cook Street, which later boasted two tiers of white porches where ladies gathered to pose for photographs before a game of croquet in its gardens—became the village centerpiece, a representation of Dannemora's economic prosperity.

The mining experiment was ultimately a failure. Clinton was too remote for major markets, and the infrastructure of the village was unequipped to handle the workload. Yet the prison had laid a foundation for what would become part of the largest industry in the North Country. In 1973, Gov. Nelson Rockefeller signed legislation to combat the urban

---

19 Clinton Prison was the facility's original name. It was later changed to Clinton Correctional Facility, though it is often still referred to as "Clinton Prison" or simply "Dannemora," after the town in which it resides.

20 The fifty inmates arrived from the now dismantled Mount Pleasant Prison in Plattsburgh, not to be confused with Mount Pleasant Correctional Facility in Iowa.

drug crisis. The laws, aimed at dealers and addicts, carried a maximum sentence of twenty-five years to life for possessing or selling relatively low quantities of heroin, morphine, opium, cocaine, and cannabis. The Rockefeller Drug Laws, as they were known, filled the courts with new criminals and sent incarceration numbers through the roof. Albany soon needed more facilities to accommodate the increasing inmate population. State Senator Ronald Stafford—a Dannemora native, the son of a corrections officer, and a powerful Republican out of Plattsburgh—saw the expansion of the prison system as a moneymaking opportunity for depressed rust belt towns in the Adirondacks. Within one decade, a staggering fourteen new state and federal facilities were built in what locals now call "CO Country."

Prisons began to create business where the private sector had failed. The value of iron ore had depreciated by the turn of the century. Small farms, factories, and mines were hit by big corporations outsourcing their materials and labor. Railroads like the old Delaware & Hudson that once ran through Dannemora eventually fell into bankruptcy. By June 2015, five other state prisons—Bare Hill, Franklin, Upstate, Altona, and Adirondack, each less than a fifty-mile drive from Dannemora—employed approximately 3,500 correctional officers and supervisors, or about 18 percent of the nearly 20,000 sergeants, lieutenants, and COs employed by DOCCS. Corrections officers and jailers made up 16.3 percent of the region's entire labor force, excluding the physicians, maintenance men, outside contractors, and other civilians that worked in the facilities. And even as a shift in philosophy toward the prison system began to take shape (by 2008, lawmakers were eager to reduce incarceration rates and consequently rejected the notion that facilities were a financial savior for underemployed upstaters), prison culture had already been deeply ingrained in Dannemora. It had become the bread and butter of the region, and therefore a way of life.

. . .

Joyce Mitchell hung up the phone and turned to Lyle.

"The state police called," she said.

Lyle looked at his wife. It was early Sunday and he had not expected *another* call from law enforcement.

"For what?" he asked.

"They want to know something about a package."

His eyes remained fixed on her. They were not filled with accusation, but with sincere disbelief.

"Package? What are you talkin' about?"

Joyce had spent the previous day at the troopers' barracks in Malone, hours after she had woken up in Alice Hyde Medical Center to text messages from her son Tobey: *What's going on? The state police called, they're looking for you.* It had taken a second or so before she remembered the events of Friday night. Lyle had driven her to the barracks where she spent hours answering questions: *Did you know about the plan? Did you help them? Did you know Matt and Sweat had escaped?*

Her answer was a firm "no," each time.

Yes, she had lied. She lied to them just like she lied to Lyle, to her family, to herself. She had been lying for months and now she was wound up in a tangled, sticky web of her own weaving. She had felt like an ugly, fat, middle-aged woman trapped in a small town. Their attention made her feel attractive. The Mexico fantasy made her feel alive.

And whether or not she had always believed it to be true, Joyce was now convinced of one thing that she felt justified this deceit: Matt would have murdered Lyle, eliminating "the glitch" in their plan to escape.

The investigators wanted to see her again, and she thought she knew why: the 2-pound frozen packages of raw hamburger meat she had pushed past security, the first containing two chisels, two concrete drill bits, and a punch; the second, hacksaw blades.

Her mind raced.

"He would've killed my husband," she thought. "He would've killed him right in front of me. He would've taken that little pair of [sewing] scissors and stabbed him."

She turned to Lyle again.

"We'll go back. I need to talk to the troopers."

• • •

In the thirty-six hours since Blair's standing count, law enforcement had flooded Dannemora in full force. There had been a grid search of the area. More than 150 leads had been developed. Uniformed investigative and specialty units had been deployed on the ground. Additional services had been applied statewide. They were considering every conceivable scenario: the convicts might be traveling together, they might have separated, they might have received assistance from the outside. The U.S. Marshals Service had issued two warrants for the inmates, each with an attached $25,000 reward. Cuomo had promised a separate $100,000 for any information that led to their apprehension and arrest. He had called it "a crisis situation for the state."

Behind the scenes, the manhunt had presented a logistical nightmare. Competing interests among local, state, and national agencies were already at play. The lack of cell and radio towers in the Adirondacks had further complicated coordination, making communication between men and women in the field and central command all but impossible. Troopers and COs had already weathered a day of thick brush and unrelenting rain. The officers had formed a perimeter along Route 374, Route 30, and Bucks Corners Road. They had stood shoulder to shoulder for hours in the downpour, staring into the wilderness.

The Adirondacks were Troop B's territory, and Maj. Charles E. Guess was the man in charge. This was his turf and it was said that he would be damned if he'd let two inmates show him up. There was only one problem: neither he nor any other leader in law enforcement had the slightest idea where the fugitives were.

• • •

Warmth from the sun washed over Sweat's back. The heat felt good on his tired body. His muscles were still thawing out after a night spent on the mountain, where the temperature, starting at a pleasant sixty, had dropped more than twenty degrees. They had set up camp where the land flattened and went about building a fire. Matt had slept for an hour and a half or so while Sweat tended to the flames. When Matt awoke Sweat tried to sleep, but thirty minutes into slumber he was startled by a rush of cold air. He turned over to see their bonfire burned to embers. Matt fed the pit with damp leaves and wet wood, causing it to smoke.

"He doesn't know how to build a damn fire!" Sweat thought, cursing to himself.

In prison, Matt had let on that he was an expert out-doorsman. But less than thirty-six hours into their journey it had become increasingly clear that he was out of his element. Sweat could already see he had overestimated his partner's abilities. He knew from the outset it would be difficult for him to adjust. (Matt was a city kid who stayed inside at even the hint of inclement weather, whereas Sweat, even as a toddler, could run out in the snow shirtless.) The endless woodland seemed to make Matt feel exposed. He had spent most of his life locked up, and the free world was a very large place.

By dawn they had cleared the site. As they made their westward descent, Sweat noticed a small wooden structure in the distance.

"Hey, is that a cabin?"

"Where?" said Matt.

"Over there."

They approached and saw that it was a deer blind, a small doorless hunter's dwelling with a rubberized roof draped in camo tarp. On the inside, a two-foot by four-foot shelf hung under two Plexiglas windows. A layer of industrial carpeting insulated the walls of the single room, though its wooden floor had all but rotted. The place had two chairs, as if it had been set up especially for them—one made of corroded metal, its seat fitted with a faded leather cushion, and the other of cheap plastic, like the kind found on a person's back porch.

There was no place to sleep except for the floor. Yet Matt did not wish to rest on such an unforgiving surface, and readily began to tear the carpet off the walls.

"We should collect some fern branches, too," he said as he lay the textile beneath their feet. "Something to make it more comfortable."

Sweat nodded. He thought it was worth putting the time into their new quarters. Monday's forecast had promised heavy showers. Depending on the length and severity of the downpour, they might be holed up here for the next few days. "Better to collect the leaves now while they're dry," he thought.

The men left the blind, pulling its canvas cover over the entryway to keep out the rain and the mosquitos that were sure to come with it. They ventured down to the narrow creek at the base of the slope to wash their blood-stained socks and shave what stubble had grown since their last grooming. When they returned, they built another fire with the brush they had gathered and charred half a pepperoni stick over the flames. As the meat tenderized, its sweet, spicy aroma mingled with the smoke from the ends of their rollies. This night was like many of the nights they had spent together in the North Yard, only this time they were not bound by the rules of Clinton. This time, they were free men.

• • •

As a teenager, Joyce had dropped out of St. Regis Falls High School to work twenty miles south at the now shuttered

Tru-Stitch Slipper Factory. At the time, she had been dating Tobey Premo, a neighborhood boy who had fallen hard for her youthful looks. The couple soon married and had a son, who carried his father's name.

It was at Tru-Stitch where Joyce had first met the company's employee Lyle Mitchell—and it was not long before rumors of an illicit romance started to swirl.

She left Premo and later married Lyle, who now steered their black Jeep out of the Malone barracks and headed west for their home in Dickinson Center. Members of B.C.I. in Troop B had questioned her for hours. Night had already fallen.

Lyle looked over at his wife in the passenger seat, still stunned by what she had revealed at the police station.

"Well how can it—how can it happen?" he asked. An investigator had pulled him aside at the barracks. "Mr. Mitchell," the officer said, "your wife has [been] more involved than she's lettin' on."

"It just—I got in over my head, and I was scared."

She paused before speaking again. He now knew about her bringing tools to Matt and Sweat, but there was more she wanted to say.

"I got something else to tell you."

"What's that?"

"Their plan was—they wanted to kill you."

"*What?*"

She explained that Matt had wanted her to pick them up outside the powerhouse. He had asked her to drive. He had offered to give her sleeping pills to give to Lyle so that he would doze off and she could leave their house unnoticed.

Joyce told him what she claimed to have told Matt: "I love my husband. I am not hurtin' him. I can't do this."

"He tried to kiss me a couple of times, but I said no," she said as they drove. "That's when he started with his threats."

Her words were met with silence.

"I love you," Joyce said. "I didn't know if you loved me anymore. It just went too far."

BINGHAMTON, NEW YORK—1985

David felt a warm liquid dripping down the backs of his legs. He hopped off his red metal tricycle and climbed the steps of the crumbling concrete stairway that led to his family's first-floor apartment.

His mother was at the door. She saw his soiled shorts and her face twisted with rage.

"You are old enough to know better!" she screamed.

David bit his lip. He felt the heat rise under his cheeks.

"It's not my fault," the boy said. His eyes remained on the floor.

The next day it happened again, this time at school. David had not noticed until several other students began to snicker. Pamela received a call to pick him up early. She took him home and told him to bend over. She raised the belt over her shoulder.

David held back tears. None of this would have happened had they not moved to Binghamton and met Paul, the thin man who lived alone in the other first-floor unit of their house on Robinson Street. He had considered Paul nice enough as far as grown-ups went; he had watched him visit with his mother on several occasions. He had been a welcome guest in their home. So when Paul had asked him to come to his apartment one afternoon, David readily accepted. He followed Paul to a bedroom in the back of the house. He asked David to lay down. David did as he was told.

Paul rolled David onto his abdomen and slipped off his pants.

The boy began to thrash.

"It's OK. Don't you trust me?" Paul said, loosening his own trousers while propping up the boy's bare bottom. David had no time to respond. Within seconds, he felt the pressure of a foreign object forcing its way deep inside.

"I don't want to! It hurts!" He cried but the words were muffled by the mattress. Paul held him firm. He assured David not to worry, the pain would pass. It would be their secret.

"Remember," Paul had said after the encounter. "Don't tell anyone."

DAY THREE

Ransom Cook, Clinton's first warden, needed strong, sturdy inmates to build the new facility and mine the mountains' iron ore. He had traveled to Auburn and Sing Sing and handpicked a crew of convicts to bring back to the Adirondacks. The new recruits cleared the land and began construction of its first cell block. They erected a kitchen, saw mill, blacksmith shop, and brass foundry. Over the next fifty years, other structures were also added, including the tuberculosis hospital, a mess hall, and an auditorium for moving pictures. One of the finest buildings came in in 1941, nearly a century after they first broke ground: the Church of St. Dismas, the Good Thief, the country's first freestanding church built on prison property, a Neo-Gothic landmark constructed by inmates from salvaged stone.[21]

---

21 The structure is also referred to as, "Church of the Good Thief" and "St. Dismas." Fr. Ambrose Hyland commissioned the structure. (Mass was previously celebrated in the auditorium, beneath the

Fires, riots, and technological advances would alter its landscape, but the bones of the prison would remain. Today, administrative buildings make up most its southern border. Cell blocks run parallel to these offices, and farther north are more blocks that flank either side of the mess hall, which sits just below Clinton's Special Housing Unit—lodging for those inmates deemed unfit to co-exist with its general population.[22] Nearby is the North Yard, about eight acres of land that consists of "The Flats," a large, level expanse of dirt at its southern edge. Here there are weight benches and barbells, and "The Club," an enclosed area where men may shower off after exercise. Farther north are "The Courts," plots of prisoner-controlled turf with picnic tables and cast-iron wood burning stoves that often fill the air with the smell of sizzling empanadas and slow-cooked venison.[23]

For twelve years Sweat had been part of this place and

---

prison's mess hall.) Its pews were fashioned from Appalachian red oak, donated by former Clinton inmate, Charles "Lucky" Luciano, and its stain glass windows were crafted by artist Carmelo Louis Soraci, who had also done time in the prison. Construction began in 1939 (the year Hyland arrived) and was completed in 1941. It is part of the National Register of Historic Places.

22 Inmates assigned to a DOCCS Special Housing Unit are generally placed in SHU because of a disciplinary infraction (i.e. bringing drugs into the facility, trying to harm another prisoner or corrections officer, etc.). SHU is also used to house inmates deemed mentally unfit to reside with other prisoners. An inmate's health status must fall in accordance with the guidelines put out by the New York State Office of Mental Health.

23 The North Yard once boasted of baseball diamonds, a football field and even a popular ski slope, which was set up in the mid-twentieth century. It was dismantled in the early nineties amid growing concerns that inmates might suffer unnecessary injury. The courts, which date back to the same time period, have endured.

the society that had evolved from within. He kept out of trouble in the North Yard, which had long been a hotbed for gangs and narcotics; the Bloods generally liked crack, the Jamaicans favored weed, and a share of the white guys took to heroin, which was said to run a man much less dough on the inside than out on the city streets. On countless occasions these drugs were brought in by visitors. (Inmates' girlfriends often stuffed condoms with cocaine and stuck the rubbers inside themselves.) Yet guards brought in drugs too, hoping to profit from Clinton's lucrative drug trade. The prison earned a reputation for its "dirty COs"—those officers who quietly broke the code of conduct they had sworn to keep. While many would faithfully abide by the rules, others had ulterior motives. For the right amount of money, a man could get almost anything he wanted in the prison, and some guards played this to their advantage.

Sweat much preferred the courts; he had managed two of his own, numbers 242 and 255. He won a third court in a raffle—No. 7, a legendary garden once managed by renowned inmate Charles "Lucky" Luciano that had been passed down to Salvatore "Sally Dogs" Lombardi, who lost the plot after authorities discovered he had a knife stashed under a bench. One of Sally's guys had approached Sweat soon after. He told him that winning a raffle changed nothing; the court was rightfully Sally's. Sweat, who had often smoked Italian sausages for the Genovese gangster, told the man not to worry. It was mere paperwork, plain and simple. The court would always belong to the capo.

Sweat had played the prison game well. He stayed out of trouble, made smart alliances, and, for the most part, kept to himself. He followed its unwritten code, one that every man at Clinton must honor should he expect to survive: stick to basic conversation ("Working out tonight? You doin' chest or legs?" or "Going to the club? You goin' now?" or "We cookin' outside? What are we havin'?"); keep clean (foul body odor invites a fight); and stay on the good side of the guards.

The crime for which he was convicted had also given him an advantage.

"What you did out there gives you a certain status," Sweat had once said. "The more severe it was, the more respect you get. You get congratulations for something that's not worth congratulating. It shouldn't be that way, but that's how it is."

In the wilderness, he could finally leave it all behind. There in the woods, Clinton and its way of life no longer mattered.

• • •

After a briefing on the situation in Dannemora Monday morning, news anchor Savannah Guthrie segued to her next guest.

"It has been nearly fifty hours since this escape took place, so these two inmates could literally be anywhere, as we just heard," she said from the set of the Today Show at Studio 1A in Rockefeller Center. "I know you have about 150 leads…that you're working. Are any in particular looking promising? How confident are you that these two will be found?"

Gov. Andrew Cuomo, live from Albany, was quick to respond.

"Well, Savannah, the first order of business is exactly that for us—to get these two escapees back into custody. They are truly dangerous, desperate men, as your report said. They are killers, they are murderers, so we want to get them back as quickly as possible. And as your report also said, they could be anywhere given this period of time. We're doing a very intensive search in the immediate area, which is basically a rural area…they could be anywhere in the country. One of them has experience in Mexico so they might even be headed south."

As he spoke, two overexposed mugshots appeared on the screen. Footage of the governor scaling a metal ladder in the bowels of Clinton rolled above the banner, "BREAKING NEWS," "MASSIVE MANHUNT FOR ESCAPED PRISONERS," and "NY GOV. CUOMO ON SEARCH & ELABORATE ESCAPE."

"Let me ask you about this," said Guthrie. "When you look at the elaborateness of this escape [route]—and I know you personally saw it—you're talking about people who acquired power tools, knew exactly how to get out, who cut through steel pipes, steel walls, shimmied down those pipes, broke through a manhole. Are they that ingenious? Are they just lucky? Or do you think they had help?"

Again, Cuomo was ready with his answer.

"I think they had help. I don't believe they could've acquired the equipment they needed to do this without help. We have a separate investigation that's going through exactly that question. You have all types of employees in a prison—"

"Help from the inside or help from the outside?" Guthrie interjected.

"Well, we're looking at everything but primarily from

the inside," Cuomo answered. "You have three types of employees in a prison: you have the guards, you have civilian employees, and then you have the private contractors who come in to do work. And we're going through the civilian employees and private contractors first. I'd be shocked if a correction guard was involved in this."

"And they left a note for guards saying, 'Have a Nice Day!' What does that tell you about their mindset?"

A slight smirk spread across the governor's face.

"A little bit—a little bit of the comedian in them. But I plan on giving them back that note, Savannah."

DAY FOUR

TUESDAY, JUNE 9TH

Sgt. Jay Cook peered into the dense foliage from the window of his rusty Crown Vic as he cruised along Chazy Lake Road, just west of the perimeter established around Dannemora. He had driven to the area on his own accord; four days into the search and he had yet to be assigned to work the manhunt. He had asked to join the detail several times, but the bosses told him to go about his normal duties.

The orders left Cook with questions that frustrated the hell out of him: "Why aren't they calling us? Why aren't they using our people who know where they heck they're goin'? Why aren't we involved in this?" The New York State Police had already dispatched one hundred personnel. Talk of bussing in more troopers from downstate had already begun to circulate—and here he was, a local sergeant with twenty-one years on the job, a known marksman who had been instructed to carry on with standard roving patrol.

Within Troop B, Cook was known as a deadeye.

Growing up he had studied how his father shot coyotes on the family dairy farm at the end of the Taylor Road in Chateaugay. From the time he was eight, Cook and his older brother Darren would climb in their father's old pick-up truck and ride out to pasture to grain their heifers. If a woodchuck crossed their path, Cook senior would take out his .22 Winchester Magnum Rimfire and tell his boys to take turns aiming at the critter. The younger Cook soon took up partridge hunting, and by his early teens ventured down to his uncle's sandpit for practice. More than fifteen years later, he displayed his skills in the qualifying exam at the New York State Police Academy. At age twenty-six, Cook had aced all three shots—the first from twenty-five yards, the second from fifteen, and the last from seven—earning a rare perfect score. The agency presented him with the Firearms Superintendent Award and an engraved Glock pistol for a job well done.

By the time Cook was thirteen, he knew he wanted to be a state trooper. Nine days after graduating from high school in 1986, he flew to San Antonio to join the U.S. Air Force. A military background might put him on the fast track to the State Police, he thought, so he went through basic training and tech school before being deployed to Little Rock, Arkansas, where the branch needed an aircraft mechanic. While still in active duty, he flew back to New York to take the trooper exam. He walked away from the test with a disappointing 84 percent, falling short of the cutoff. A number of jobs later—he had served in the Air National Guard in Burlington, V.T., held a part-time gig in the sheriff's department, and worked as a corrections officer at Green Haven Correctional Facility—Cook took the trooper exam again. This time he earned a 97. It was enough: in April 1994, he entered the New York State Police Academy. Five years later he became a firearms instructor.

Cook would tell each of his new students that a good shot with an open sighted weapon relied on two fundamental principles: sight alignment and trigger control. "Line up your sights," he would say, referring to the three boxes on the top of the pistol that help a shooter home in on the target. "If you close one eye and you focus on the top of that front sight, your body should automatically center it in the rear sight, and all you've got to do is make sure it's level across the top. When you're ready to shoot, you slowly squeeze that trigger. You don't mash it, you keep that steady, keep focusing on that front sight. Your target will be slightly blurry in the distance because you're focusing on the top sight the whole time. Then you squeeze the trigger and it goes off. If you try to make the gun go off when you think you want it to go off, that's bad. Make it a slow pull, it should actually surprise you slightly when the gun goes off."

Cook had holstered his .45 GAP Tuesday morning like he did every day on the job. As he scanned the thick brush along Chazy Lake Road, he could not help but wonder if he would eventually have to use it.

• • •

Sweat walked west following the flow of a creek, which, had he had a pole, would have been the perfect place to fish. During his stroll, he came across a beaver dam three tiers tall made of timber, mud, and stone. He admired the handiwork; he too wished to build a home with his own hands, one out here in the woods with a glass roof that could slide open for a better view of the great expanse above.

As he continued along he came across two five-gallon buckets and a patch of fertile ground that appeared to have been recently tilled. "Probably part of an old pot growing spot," he thought. Marijuana plants flourished in the foothills of the Adirondacks. (The finest weed in the state, as some locals would proudly say—and, as a few put it, their best-selling crop other than the region's abundance of cow's corn.) Figuring he could use the buckets to collect water, Sweat carried them back to the deer blind. He and Matt had been forced to stay put because of the downpour, though this suited them well enough; their feet were still recovering, and Matt's boots were barely holding up. He had purchased a new pair before leaving Clinton, but, for reasons Sweat could not quite understand, had chosen to put on the ones worse for wear.

They hoped that by tomorrow the rain would stop, and they could continue their journey in search of freedom and better shoes.

• • •

Forty miles southeast, the beating of blades sounded overhead. A tip had come in that the fugitives might be in Willsboro, New York, a town bordered by Lake Champlain on the eastern edge of the state. A resident had reported seeing two suspicious men run from a gully on Middle Road into the woods. Officers had followed up. By early afternoon, more than 440 troopers and COs in dark blue ball caps and bulletproof vests had swarmed the area. They set up checkpoints and roadblocks along NY 22. They combed the surrounding farmland. They plodded through rain-soaked pastures dotted with dairy cows. They teamed up by the dozens, searching trailers, barns, and tool sheds.

Hours passed. Dusk began to descend. By 6 p.m., they had pulled out. The trail had gone cold.

BINGHAMTON, NEW YORK—1989

In the months before turning nine, David had dealt with a number of issues at his new school, Woodrow Wilson Elementary, which sat at the top of a slope behind his Baxter Street home. The worst was when several classmates had tossed him in a grocery cart and sent the buggy down the hill. (Even though it had been a few years since he moved away from Paul—who he never told anyone about—David was still soiling his drawers, drawing taunts among his peers.) To fend off the threat of bruises and black eyes, he began to bring his Swiss Army knife to school. He started to skip class, which prompted a number of beatings from his mother, who now used a belt embellished with racecar cutouts to do the job. Each slap caused his skin to swell, forming red, auto-like welts that resembled a "NASCAR pile-up," as David later liked to think of it. Yet even after school let out for the summer, these months offered little reprieve. He spent much of his time at home with his older sister Tilly, who tortured him with girlish nicknames and other acts of aggression. After a particularly bad quarrel between the siblings, David had taken a handful of steak knives from his mother's kitchen and placed them underneath

Tilly's covers with their points up, expecting that she might flop on the mattress without ever pulling back the blanket.

(She pulled back the blanket.)

The Sweats eventually moved again, from Baxter to nearby Liberty Street. David transferred out of Woodrow Wilson to a Boards of Cooperative Educational Services school two hours north in Oswego, New York, then to Pennsylvania to live with his Uncle Bernie. (He had enjoyed his time there, although the stay would be brief. David had overheard a conversation between Bernie and his wife about moving the family to Florida. Angered by the thought of another change, he decided to steal his uncle's Chevrolet Camaro and, after a joyride in the schoolyard, crashed the vehicle into a guard rail. Bernie, who liked working on the sports car as well as his Bigfoot monster truck, had had enough, and sent the boy back to Binghamton.) David then went to live with his Grandma Tuttle before being placed in Haskins Group Home, part of the Children's Home of the Wyoming Conference. These stays were interrupted by a string of foster care homes and stints back with his mother.

During this time, he intermittently saw his cousin Jeffrey Nabinger, whose family had returned to Binghamton after moving to Oklahoma. A troublemaker with a gift for story-telling, Jeff would take charge of recounting their adventures. ("It was better to be the subject of a story than to be the one telling it," David would later say. "If you were the subject, you were important. You were respected.") To anyone who would listen, Jeff narrated the blow-by-blow of the time they had burglarized a Frito Lay truck: the boys, accompanied by David's sister, Anna, and her friend, Joy, stopped at a store. Jeff had stolen a box of Slim Jims and a six-pack of Coors. Not to be outdone, David raided the truck of several small bags of chips, which Anna stuffed in her backpack. The incident landed David in Broome County Juvenile Court. It was also during this time that David, Jeff, and Jeff's brother, Mike Benedict, began to steal cars. (Mike had once taken a Monte Carlo, David a new Ford Taurus. The kids were caught, but it did not prevent David from swiping a beige commercial van the following day.)

For all the trouble they caused him, David had friends for the first time in his life. "Not good friends, mind you, but what the hell difference did it mean to me," he once said. "I didn't know the difference between good and bad friends as I never really had any. And like anyone else, you always long for acceptance."

DAY FIVE

WEDNESDAY, JUNE 10TH

Walter "Pete" Light came from a proud line of Dannemora men. He lived in the wooden house with the wooden porch on Emmons Street, built in 1895 and first owned by the Van Gorder family, then the Cosgroves, before it was passed down to his father and finally to him. And like his father, Light too had worked at Clinton, where for thirty years he has served the state as a corrections officer. Yet his fascination with the prison began well before he joined their ranks. (At age twenty-one, Light had walked past the old Warden's Residence as it was being torn down. He asked a construction worker for one of the lightning rods that had topped the late-nineteenth-century manor. The acquisition began a nearly fifty-year love affair with preserving prison artifacts.)

As the official village historian, Light knew the fugitives had been the first to escape the Main in the penitentiary's 152-year history. What he did not understand was why they were the subject of such interest. There were others who had successfully broken out of Clinton—like inmate no. 13344, Lajama Mados, a convicted murderer who, on October 7, 1920, fled from Clinton's former prison chapel. Then there was Edward Blowers, who, on Aug. 11, 1919, had jumped out of a train while being transported from Sing Sing Prison. And then there was six-foot four-inch burglar Eckert Kelly who, on July 2, 1922, simply walked out of the facility's tuberculous hospital. None of them were ever captured.

Other, more famous prison breaks became a frequent topic of discussion in the days after June 6, 2015. The fugitives out of Dannemora were likened to John Dillinger—once America's no. 1 desperado who, in 1934, was freed from a jailhouse in Lima, Ohio, by three friends, men who had broken out of Indiana State Prison the month before. Other comparisons were made to Alcatraz inmates Frank Lee Morris and brothers John and Clarence Anglin. These men had placed dummies in their beds and, in the middle of the night, slipped through vent holes in the back of their cells—concealed by paintings of grates that blended into the wall—before climbing down a drainpipe. Alcatraz itself imposed only the first obstacle: the trio had to survive the cold, shark-ridden waters of the San Francisco Bay. Morris found a solution in the March 1962 issue of the periodical *Popular Mechanics,* which featured the article, "Your Life Preserver—How will it behave if you need it?" The piece provided instructions for how to make a floatation device out of raincoats, which is just what the inmates did. (*Popular Mechanics* also happened to be Sweat's favorite magazine, which he consulted before absconding from Clinton.) Perhaps the most frequent comparison was, somewhat surprisingly, to a fictional event: *The Shawshank Redemption*, a film based on Stephen King's narrative of a prisoner who, while serving two consecutive life sentences at the imagined Shawshank State Penitentiary, spent nineteen years chiseling a tunnel out of his cell that led to the prison's sewage pipe.

Of the more than five hundred photos in Light's collection, he had none of the prisoners who had escaped—nor would he really want them.

"They don't mean nothing to me," Light said. "I don't want to say it by sayin' it, but they're just inmates."

• • •

By Wednesday morning the rain had finally passed, leaving Matt and Sweat free to explore an ATV trail not too far from the deer blind. After washing up they left their things and set out, not knowing where the path would lead.

Less than a mile later they came upon a dirt road wide enough for a standard-sized vehicle. A white trailer surrounded by waist-high grass came into view, as did a well-kept lodge, its lawn recently mowed. Sweat and Matt headed for the mobile home first, which appeared to be vacant—yet they approached it from behind just to be sure. Long, wet blades of overgrown grass had crept up and flattened against its oxidized surface. Sweat surveyed the structure with great attention but could see no signs of any alarms, nor a generator to provide it power. Satisfied that no one had been there in some time, the men pressed their faces to the glass. They could make out a television, DVD player, and satellite box, as well as a few pieces of furniture and a pantry, which held the promise of provisions.

Matt tried the back door first.

"Locked," he said, giving the knob another good twist just to be sure.

Sweat went around to the front door. To his surprise, it swung right open.

The place was a sizable one, complete with kitchenette, bathroom, and bunkroom. Seeing several useful items laying out, Sweat and Matt removed the fabric cases from nearby pillows and began to raid the cupboards and countertops, placing things in the sacks like two kids collecting candy on Halloween. Crackers, coffee packets, tea, toilet paper, matches, gum, hot sauce, and hand wipes all went in, along with a few leftovers from half-consumed MREs, or "Meals Ready-to-Eat"—a nutrient-dense pre-packaged emergency food supply carried by hunters and members of the military. Sweat and Matt each took a knife and Sweat, seeing a knife sharpener, white cord, and cardboard, took those items too, hoping they might come in handy.

"Hey, look! I found boots but they're too big," Matt said from the other side of the room, holding up the shoes before tossing them to the side.

Sweat went to reach for the boots. "Well, in that case—"

"No!" Matt protested. "Those are for me!"

"I thought you said they were too big!" Sweat said, laughing. "Put them on if you're going to take them. And take your old ones back with us, we can't leave anything of ours here." Not wishing to linger any longer, they stuffed their packs with blankets, blue jeans, camo pants, two long sleeve shirts, Band-Aids, toilet paper, and a pair of green wool gloves, and headed back to camp.

Upon returning to the blind, the pungent scent of black pepper filled their nostrils.

"Boy, does that make the deer blind smell pretty!" said Sweat. He had doused their belongings in the seasoning earlier to throw any curious bloodhounds off course. The spice now mixed with the scent of citronella, which Sweat had also nicked from the trailer to ward off the thousands of biting bugs that had bred during the days of heavy rainfall. Wielding his new knife, he sliced up Matt's old leather boots, and from the scraps fashioned a pair of sheaths. (It was in his nature to make do with what was available, and he could not let good material go to waste. Sometimes, as a child, he would tinker with items like a television, taking it apart piece by piece before putting the machine back together. Through these explorations Sweat learned how things worked and, if the item was beyond repair, what parts could be saved. He had a natural ability for seeing stuff beyond its intended purpose. To him, a boot was never just a boot.)

Matt and Sweat passed the afternoon at the blind before venturing out again. This time, they made for the clubhouse.

Sweat went around to the side door while Matt stayed out front. The former examined this entrance for a moment or so when he noticed a key dangling from a hook on the wall next to the jamb.

"What the hell, why not?" Sweat thought. He removed the key and pushed it into the lock. The mechanism clicked and he nudged the door open.

Upon entering, he saw Matt standing in the cabin.

"How the hell did you get in?!"

"The front door was unlocked," he said with a grin.

Sweat smiled. "They left this for me," he said, holding up the key.

He made his way up the stairs to a single large room with a storage cabinet, along with several dressers and beds, enough sleeping space to house a small group of hunters quite comfortably. He lifted each of the mattresses, squatting down to see if any rifles had been stowed on the springs for safe keeping. Sweat found none, but rummaging through several storage bins yielded a transistor radio, a few batteries, and Leatherman knife.

As he inspected these findings, he heard Matt's voice come from somewhere behind him.

"Hey, look at this!"

Sweat wheeled around to see Matt kneeling beside a hard plastic case on the other side of the room. "Bet they have some nice handguns in here!"

Matt's face dropped as soon as he unlatched the trunk: inside was a set of premium grilling utensils.

Disheartened, he went back downstairs; the only things he had found so far were a few coins and some loose bullets. (What he was going to do with this stuff Sweat could only guess, but Matt appeared to regard them as small treasures, and that alone seemed to negate the disappointment of the cookware.) When he reached the landing, he found Sweat in the kitchen digging through the cabinets for food, and so decided to have a look in the refrigerator.

"Dave, there's a bunch of beer in the fridge."

"I know." Sweat had already looked inside. "Let's grab a few apiece."

They gathered all the tallboys they could carry and, with their belongings packed, they closed the door of the clubhouse.

Night had fallen by the time they went back outside. It had grown so dark that Matt could not see his hand stretched out in front of him.

"I think we've missed the trail," he whispered, his voice rising an octave.

"No we haven't," said Sweat. They were still too close to the cabin and too close to the main road to risk pulling out the flashlights. "We're almost there."

The even, hard-packed road eventually gave way to a gritty, irregular surface, indicating they had reached the ATV trail. Once they were into the woods, they illuminated the path ahead until they reached the blind. Their body heat had warmed the beers, so Sweat submerged the tallboys in a bucket of cold spring water. He then went about building a fire with the logs he had gathered earlier that day and placed them against a wall of river rocks he had built to serve as a barrier against the wind.

Both he and Matt were pleased with their day's work. Apart from the knife, radio, batteries, and pocket change, they had also procured two cans of tuna fish, a cooking pot, an emergency foil thermal blanket, one can of sweet green peas, three cans of Vienna sausage, a few candles, one flashlight, some more knives, a bag of honey-roasted peanuts, and several jars of pickles. Cracking open a Michelob Light, Sweat pulled up a seat—one of the white buckets he had found the morning before—and began to divvy the loot, listening to the radio and dining on the sausage, peas, and pepperoni, smoked over the fire and flavored with Tabasco sauce.

Matt turned to Sweat. His freedom had finally begun to sink in.

"This is the life. Let's just stay here."

Sweat smiled, and they talked for a minute or so before a voice on the radio interrupted the conversation: *Joyce Mitchell, a civilian worker at Clinton Correctional Facility, will likely face charges for assisting two inmates' escape from the prison...*

Matt's ears perked up. He looked at Sweat, who listened intently.

The broadcaster said Joyce told investigators she had provided Sweat and Matt tools and had knowledge of their plan.

Sweat felt a twinge of remorse, but he did not feel he and Matt were to blame. Had she done what she was supposed to do—what she had *promised* to do—she would not be in this predicament. (And they'd all be a hell of a lot farther along and be much more comfortable at that.) Yet he knew what this now meant: Joyce would most likely be committed to a life like the one they had left behind.

A second news update put thoughts of the prison scamstress out of his head: the announcer said the search for the inmates had turned to Cadyville.

"Where the hell is that? Sweat said.

Matt shrugged. "Dunno."

As if the voice from the radio had heard them, it promptly explained: Cadyville was a town southeast of Dannemora, a good twenty miles plus from their current location.

"Ha!" Matt laughed. He held up a tallboy and tapped Sweat's in triumph. Tonight, they would be able to sleep in peace.

DAY SIX

Michael McCaffrey spent Thursday morning making the final preparations for his medieval fantasy wedding, which was set to take place in two days' time. He and his fiancée, Terry Ann, would get married in a venue fit for the Middle Ages: the woods of Memorial Recreation Park in Malone. Almost everything had been taken care of; he had appointed the court jester (his cousin, Josh Gero), selected the friar (friend Kevin Pentalow), and gathered a band of local merry men (more friends of the couple).

Yet as McCaffrey assembled the last parts of his suit of armor (which he would wear for the occasion) he could not help but wonder if his nuptials would be attended by two unexpected guests.

Like many of his neighbors, McCaffrey had become engrossed in every detail of the prison break. He frequently tuned into News 5 Plattsburgh for updates; he read articles put out by the *Malone Telegram* and the *Plattsburgh*

Press-Republican; he participated in dozens of Facebook discussions about goings-on in Dannemora. Some people on social media—the anti-government, anarchist types, as he called them—cheered on the fugitives. Others, like him, wanted the inmates caught. Yet despite the differences of opinion, one thing was clear to the thirty-eight-year-old man from Malone: the escape had brought a certain level of excitement that his hometown had never seen before.

McCaffrey had given the prison little thought over the years. The first time he had seen Clinton Correctional Facility was as a kid on a trip to Plattsburgh with his parents. "What is that place?" he had asked his father as he looked out the window at the whitewashed wall and its formidable watchtowers, nestled in the side of the mountain. "Is that a castle?" His father shook his head. "No," he had said. "That's the prison."

Years later, while working as a vendor for the local food and supply distributor, North Country Candy & Gifts, which serviced the area's correctional facilities with products like shoe polish, shoe strings, toques, do-rags, and cans of chewing tobacco, he went behind the wall.[24] That visit left a lasting impression: the prison and its grounds felt alien, and the inmates, who watched him as he unloaded the boxes from his gold Chevy Impala, made six-foot four-inch, 270-pound McCaffrey feel uneasy.

He had a similar feeling now as he thought back to the photo of Matt in his green prison uniform. Of course, he

24 A "toque" is a French-Canadian term for a tight-fitting knit cap. (In France, the word includes other types of headwear.) New Yorkers who live close to the border often use this term, which is also spelled, "tuque."

wouldn't want to meet either him or Sweat in the woods. Yet he swore there was something wicked in Matt's sly smile—something sinister *behind* his dark eyes—that made even a big guy like him afraid.

As McCaffrey surveyed his armor, he hoped the fugitives would find another party to crash.

• • •

Greg Durandetto barely recognized the face of the hardened man splashed across his television screen. It bore little resemblance to the Richard Matt he knew from growing up in Tonawanda, New York—the mischievous "ballbuster" who passed his time playing hooky, pulling practical jokes, and picking up girls.

"He wasn't always this murderer," Durandetto said. "He wasn't like that. We started as kids being stupid in summer Bible school. I went on to working at a local plant and he went on to prison. I still don't know what happened."

Durandetto first met Matt—or Ricky, as he calls him—during those Bible school days. He had taken to him immediately, as he said most people did; Matt's smooth, olive skin paired well with his thick dark hair and lean physique, and his clean-cut appeal and impish charm won him favor with teenage girls. Their years in Tonawanda High School would be marked by a series of tomfooleries: the summer days they spent landscaping Tonawanda City Cemetery on Main Street, smacking each other with weed whackers; the time Matt stole a boat, which he later learned belonged to the town judge; the day he stole dozens of shoes from a store and set them out on the front lawn of city hall; and the night he nicked a police officer's uniform and wore it while barhopping on Elmwood Avenue.

"Imagine that!" Matt had said at one watering hole that evening, posing for pictures with female patrons. "Chicks dig guys in uniforms!"

"Yeah," Durandetto had groaned. "We're so going to jail!"

"He was just one funny son of a bitch," Durandetto said years after that outing. "Rick was also a street-smart guy. He was quick to pick up on things and learn things. He could eye people up. He was a good talker. He knew how to handle himself with women, with anybody. He used to like to impress people because he didn't have nothing."

Matt spent most of his childhood in foster care with what Durandetto said was "little direction." He longed to have the life that belonged to his friends, a life with parents and a stable home. (Matt had been the first of their friends to have his own apartment—a sweltering small room on Hill Place Road where he entertained guests with grilled cheese sandwiches, toasted on a hot plate by the edge of his bed.) He later married Vee Marie Harris and had two children, Nick and Francesca, an attempt to create the family he had not been given at birth.

But somewhere along the way the young man Durandetto knew had become someone else.

"When he got into drugs it changed him," he said. "He was with the wrong crowd, the wrong people. When he was with me, he was Rick Matt. He was a Tonawanda kid. When he was with these other guys, he had to show he was a hard ass.

"That's when he distanced himself from me. He went one way; I went the other. And he lost his way."

• • •

Corrections officers lined the edge of Bucks Corners Road. Fixed posts had been placed along Route 374, eight miles of which were shut down after bloodhounds were thought to have picked up a scent. More than five hundred state troopers and other members of law enforcement had been brought in to man the roadblocks, search the area, and follow up on complaints. Residents were advised to stay inside, lock the doors, and keep their porch lights on.

By Thursday, Cook had officially been assigned to the detail. He reported to the state police satellite office in Dannemora that morning before heading out. While driving along Bucks Corners, he received a transmission of a sighting not too far from his location.

He went up to several COs on his stretch of the road.

"You hear that? Think they have an active track going?" he asked them.

The officers all shook their heads. Six days of rain, bug bites, lack of sleep, and fruitless leads had lowered their morale.

Cook, however, was fresh on the job. He wanted answers. He wanted to find these men.

• • •

Sweat began to pack up at the deer blind, placing food and toiletries into his guitar case. He and Matt took two knives each, but left behind the other blades, along with a cooking pot, three cans of Labatt and Coors Light, and the loose bullets Matt had proudly collected.

Heading slightly south, then west down the mountain, they skirted the pond and beaver dam Sweat had admired a few days before. (They had put in many miles since Dannemora; at least twenty but maybe more, as it was difficult to tell in the deep woods under the dense canopy just how far they had walked. Trees, bushes, bramble, it all started to look the same, so much so that, at times, they even ended up walking in circles.) The two held a steady pace until afternoon showers slowed their descent. Matt pulled the emergency foil blanket over their heads, but it did little to keep them dry. Sweat's fingers could barely bend, frozen from the steady rush of foothill rainfall. The ground water had risen as high as their ankles as they waded through the deluge. Unable to continue like this, they stopped to construct a shelter from tree limbs—though this too proved to be useless.

"We can't stay here," Sweat said over the cracking thunder as the earth sunk beneath his feet. "It's all mud. We need to move."

Carrying the pile of branches, they relocated to an old stone quarry where the ground was firm. Here, they collected a number of flat rocks for the floor of the fort, flipping each one so that the dry side faced up. It turned out to be a decent structure, yet the cold wind and icy rain still rushed through. They huddled tightly together, shoulder to shoulder, the thermal foil blanket draped over their backs.

Matt pulled out two long candle sticks he had taken from the lodge and, using a lighter to ignite the wick, handed one to Sweat. The flame put out little heat, though in this weather, some warmth was better than none. Sweat soon nodded off, only to be jolted awake to the sensation of hot dripping wax.

His body trembled as he relit the tip. He was sure this was coldest he had ever been.

DAY SEVEN

FRIDAY, JUNE 12TH

For the past seven days, Clinton Correctional Facility had been on lockdown. The mess hall was closed, programs were suspended, industry work was postponed, phone privileges were revoked, recreation in the yards had been banned—and the COs were now on edge.

It had been a tortuous week for the guards. Many were humiliated by the escape. Some were ashamed to work at the prison. Others had grown increasingly anxious that the investigation was shifting from finding the inmates to goings-on behind Clinton's perimeter wall. For years, they had operated in near isolation. Now they would be under Albany's microscope. The governor's patience had worn thin when he visited the Honor Block. A few people said they had heard the politician call out inmate Patrick Alexander as he passed his cell next to the now vacant A6-22: "They must have kept you awake with all that cuttin', huh? Let me guess, you don't know fucking nothin'."

Cuomo's alleged statement was believed to have had dire consequences for the prisoner. According to those familiar with the event, several hours after the governor's visit, a few officers carried Alexander away in shackles. Whispers soon spread that he was held up by the throat as they pummeled his face, pumping him for information on the fugitives before dragging his swollen, bloodied body back to its quarters. Others were rumored to have received similar treatment. Some were allegedly choked. Several were sent to solitary confinement. At least one claimed a guard had thrown a bag over his head and threatened to waterboard him.

Clinton had a long history of such transgressions. In the prison's early days, disobedient men were tied up and beat with a leather paddle. Some were given shocks of electricity. Others were whipped. By the turn of the century, cell blocks were becoming increasingly overcrowded, and living conditions started to deteriorate. On July 22, 1929, in a desperate attempt to flee, 1,300 prisoners charged the perimeter wall. They set fire to the buildings and threw stones at the guards. (Because of this, the riot would later be known as "the rock concert.") Cops, game wardens, and border patrol officers were brought in to quell the protests. The state police stormed the gate to drive back the inmates. By early morning, three men had perished in the quest for freedom as Clinton burned in the background.

Then there was the case of forty-four-year-old Leonard Strickland. COs said this man, who was schizophrenic, was being "non-compliant" on October 3, 2010. They cuffed him, brought him into a room, and put him in the corner. The officers said Strickland was "pushing off the wall," resisting their efforts to restrain him. He sunk to the floor where guards picked him up by the wrists—still cuffed, his arms hyperextended behind his back—and dragged his limp body out of the room. The inmate eventually lost consciousness. Medics were called to resuscitate him, but it was too late. Strickland was pronounced dead due to insufficient oxygen to his heart. The episode was captured by the prison's security cameras, and the guards later admitted they did not check his pulse, nor did they make sure was still breathing after they knocked him out. No charges were ever brought against the COs.

Corrections officers had their work cut out for them at Clinton, where inmates had a reputation for being some of the state's most dangerous criminals. (A few notable prisoners include Ralph "Bucky" Phillips, who had escaped from another facility and killed a state trooper while on the run; Altemio Sanchez, known as the "Bike Path Rapist" for slaying three women and forcing himself upon twenty others; and John Jamelske, dubbed the "Syracuse Dungeon Master" for kidnapping women and keeping them as sex slaves.) But beatings at the hands of COs (which often resulted in black eyes, cracked teeth, and broken bones) were fairly common occurrences. Many of the guards, as many inmates would later say, never committed such acts—yet they too were complicit. These COs turned a blind eye to such treatment, prisoners contended, which only escalated after the discovery of two empty beds on the Honor Block. And in the days after the escape, some would say, it became even more difficult to tell who the real criminals were.

• • •

By morning, the storm had finally passed, yet a palpable dampness still hung in the air. Sweat crawled out of the lean-to, his limbs stiff from hours crouched on the quarried stones. He and Matt shook off the moisture and removed their sodden socks to wring out the rainwater.

A few minutes later, with their boots laced up and bags packed, they took to the trail—but by 10 a.m., Matt had already begun to tire.

"I've got to stop," he said.

Sweat pointed to a boulder up ahead. "Let's go right up there and you can sit and rest." He pulled out the bag of peanuts and tossed them over. They had only had one granola bar each that morning, hardly enough for how far they had hiked. "Here, take a handful. And drink some water too."

The sustenance held Matt over for several more miles, until the two men approached a cliff with large stone blocks strewn at its base. They set out to climb the crag, which at first seemed easy enough. Yet as they moved upward the land became muddy, and their boots slipped on the sludge. Matt reached the top first, with relative ease. (Sweat struggled a bit, but he was also the one carrying most of their supplies.)

Slightly out of breath, Matt and Sweat stood up to behold a humbling view: a layer of leafy green, glistening large lakes, and winding country roads. They were so high up that their eyes seemed level with the peaks of the surrounding mountains.

Sweat beamed. "Let's see them follow that trail."

The men sat to rest again, but they were quickly interrupted by the sound of a chopper, its blades beating somewhere over the canopy. Not wishing to be seen, they took to walking once more.

By midday they came across the charred remains of a cabin; a fire, it seemed, had swept through, leaving nothing but the foundation. There they changed into fresh clothes and let their boots, shirts, and socks air out in the summer breeze. Matt slept off the afternoon, while Sweat laid back and let the daylight wash over his skin, damp from perspiration. At around dinner time they gathered their things and followed the light of the falling sun, its orange and yellow rays streaking across the blue expanse like the paint strokes in one of Matt's landscapes.

"It would be easier if we had a compass," said Matt, watching the sky as the colors dimmed. Sweat nodded. The device would not be foolproof, as the ore of the mountains could affect its magnetic arrow, but a compass would still be a good thing to have. Clouds had obscured the stars over the past few nights, and moss was not always detectable in the dark, making it difficult to know which way was west.

That night, when they picked up and began to hike again, whether by coincidence or by the mystic force of the woods, their request was granted: the path soon led them to an elevated tree stand where, after climbing its ladder, Sweat found a perfect, pocket-sized ball compass.[25]

"You've got to be fucking kidding me!" he said, looking down at the center of the floor at the object. "We were just saying we needed one! I can't believe it's just sitting here!"

Further inspection of the area revealed that the path would hit a dead end, so they went back the way they came. "You know, I don't even care," Sweat said as they made for a

---

25 A tree stand is a small enclosure on stilts. It looks similar to a tree house and is used by hunters to give them a better vantage point.

main road, which they had passed before taking the trail to the tree stand. "The compass was worth the [extra] walk."

After dark, they crossed this road and went deeper into the forest. Yet twenty minutes of tripping over roots and being scratched by pricker bushes had slowed their pace, forcing them to travel along the paved route. Occasionally the headlights of an oncoming car—which, as Sweat put it, served as "a warning beacon like you wouldn't believe"— forced them to jump off to the side. They went on like this, dodging the bright beams, until they saw what appeared to be homes in the distance where the road veered north. They took the first westbound trail they came across, then moved to another trail that opened up into a large field.

Sweat could not help but marvel at the sky above. The stadium lights in the North Yard had drowned out the stars. Tonight it was clear, the clearest it had been since they had set out from Clinton one week ago, and he could not remember a time when they had shone with such brilliance.

• • •

Joyce Mitchell stood before Judge Mark Rogers in Plattsburgh City Court, a red two-story complex on the edge of Lake Champlain, south of the Cumberland Bay. The time was just after 11 p.m.

"Miss Mitchell," Judge Rogers said. "You're here for purposes of being arraigned."

She raised her chin, but her eyes did not meet his. Her shoulders slumped slightly forward, her hands folded in front, her wrists cuffed to a black belt around her waist. Her lime green t-shirt, its brightness accentuated by the fluorescent lights overhead, drew every eye in her direction, a punctuation mark in the otherwise stark room. Word of her arrest had traveled swiftly that evening. Reporters packed the wooden pews. They sat in silence, waiting to hear the indictment.

"All right, the defendant is charged here with two offenses, including misdemeanor criminal facilitation in the fourth degree and felony of promoting prison contraband in the first degree, the criminal facilitation charge being in violation of Section 115 Subdivision one of the penal law and the contraband charge being in violation of Section 205.25, Subdivision one of the penal law of the State of New York," said Rogers. "Do you waive a more formal reading of those charges, Mr. Bruno?"

"Yes, Your Honor," said Keith Bruno, who stood close to his client. "We acknowledge receipt of both complaints."

The lawyer already knew the details drawn up in the documents: Senior Investigator Kurt Taylor of the New York State Police had found reason to believe that on or about the first day of May 2015 at approximately 12 p.m., the prison seamstress intentionally, knowingly, and unlawfully brought chisels, a punch, a screwdriver bit, and hacksaw blades into Clinton Correctional Facility. According to the paperwork, she introduced this contraband to David Sweat and Richard Matt, providing them the means to commit the felony of escape in the first degree.

"At this time we waive the reading of complaints with respect to a not guilty plea to both charges," Bruno said.

"All right," said the judge. "And with respect to the matter of timing here—with regard to preliminary hearing?"

"We would reserve our right to a hearing Your Honor,

and ask for an adjournment of this matter to Monday morning at the regular court's time so I may have an opportunity to meet with my client to discuss this matter in [greater] detail."

Joyce remained silent throughout the exchange. Her eyes appeared glazed over, as if part of her was somewhere else.

"All right. Mr. Wylie, would you want to be heard on the issue of bail?"

Clinton County District Attorney Andrew Wylie, who stood at another table a few feet away, looked up at the bench. The DA, a tall thin man in his early fifties with gray-blue eyes and a short clean haircut, appeared confident in what he was about to say.

"Yes, Your Honor," he said. "The people would ask the court to impose the following amount in bail: $100,000 cash or $200,000 bond."

Joyce's head fell once more.

"Do you want to allocate that between the two offenses?"

"No, Your Honor," said Wylie, who asked for an additional $50,000 to $100,000 cash for the misdemeanor charge.

Rogers looked at each party before speaking again.

"We will put the matter over to Monday morning at 8:30. The defendant will be remanded in custody with the county sheriff for purposes of holding until that time. Bail will be set in the amount of $100,000 cash, $200,000 bond on the felony and $10,000 cash and $20,000 bond on the misdemeanor. And the record will reflect that you, Mr. Bruno, are assigned to represent the defendant and submission of a form regarding her financial eligibility for that assignment."

Bruno and Wylie thanked the judge. Joyce lowered her eyes as officers escorted her out of the courtroom and the reporters dashed outside to call in what had just transpired.

DAY EIGHT

SATURDAY, JUNE 13TH

At 6 a.m., Cook reported to Dannemora Elementary
School in the village community center on Emmons Street.
The state police and other agencies had set up headquarters
in the school's small gymnasium, where higher-ups briefed
them every morning on the status of the manhunt. More
than 800 state, local, and federal members of law enforcement were now part of the search, and at least 700 leads
had been developed. After the meeting, Cook gathered his
team. The sergeant jotted down each of their car numbers
and took account of who was paired up with whom before
heading out.

Cook rode with his partner, Sgt. Rich White. The
two first worked together nabbing drunk drivers in the
late nineties before Cook was transferred to Ray Brook,
New York, where he was asked to test weapons as part of
the state's "CoBIS" program—an "easy" nine-year post of
blasting bullets into a barrel that White, a distinguished

man several years Cook's senior, still gave him sass for.[26] (A few years back Cook and White had learned they were distant cousins, which only increased the good-humored banter between them.)

As they drove, both expressed their aggravation with how the operation was being handled. Frustrations had mounted over the last week because of problems in communication and the inevitable chaos it created with coordinating hundreds of personnel. The men and women from downstate did not know the area. When it came to designated duties, there was a lack of continuity from day to day; one shift they could be working a fixed post, the next they could be out vetting complaints, making the process increasingly inefficient. Morale was low among the officers, and the enthusiasm for catching the inmates had therefore begun to dwindle.

For the sergeants, the prospect of finding the fugitives was the one thing that kept them going.

"Man, can you imagine if we saw one of them running across that field right there?" Cook said to his partner as

26 The Combined Ballistic Identification System or "CoBIS" was an effort by New York to trace guns used in criminal activity. It sought to create a databank of ballistic samples taken from all new firearms sold in the state. Ballistic samples—shell casings of a bullet or projectile discharged from a specific, identified pistol or revolver— were required to be collected by firearm manufacturers, authorized dealers and anyone in the business of supplying firearms before the weapon could be sold. Instated under Gov. George Pataki's administration in 2000, CoBIS ended up being a costly program with a major flaw: it did not account for the sale of illegal weapons, which are predominately used in criminal activity. It was ultimately considered a failure and was dismantled in 2012.

they drove past the passing landscape. "Wouldn't that be awesome if we could be the ones to get him?"

• • •

Sweat woke with a start. Through the darkness, he ran his fingers over the ground, feeling the tread of tires etched in the dirt. They had left the field and moved on to the road, where they sat down for what was only supposed to be a quick break. Instead, they had nodded off.

"Come on, dude!" Sweat shook Matt's shoulder until he stirred. It was 3 a.m. They did not have much time before dawn. "We gotta go, we can't sleep in the road!"

Matt lumbered to his feet, his body heavy with exhaustion. Sweat was already standing. They had not slept long, but it was enough for him. He had been born with the gift of natural athleticism and boundless energy. With little conditioning, Sweat could sprint a good distance. One of his friends from adolescence later joked that Sweat did not even need shoes, as he seemed to run much faster without footwear. He likened him to an Olympic track star—a speeding bullet that could outrun just about anything or anyone.

This morning, however, he slowed his pace for Matt, who followed him deeper into the woods. They walked along a dirt trail for some time until they came across a lodge with a long drive. Fresh tire tracks had been pressed into the forest floor, so they decided to keep it moving. A little farther up, road signs that read "POSTED PRIVATE PROPERTY" and "NO TRESPASSING" had been tacked to the surrounding trees.

"Good," Sweat thought. "Privacy is what we want."

As they moved closer, a one-room cabin with two outhouses and a shed came into view. Two four wheelers were parked on the property, one of which had an attached trailer covered with a tarp. Sweat lifted the canvas and found it was full of fertilizer.

"Man, someone has a big garden up here," he thought. He then went over to the ATV and lifted one of its seats. A small pile of papers had been stashed there, including the owner's registration. According to these documents, the quad was licensed to a man in Cadyville.

"No fucking way," he said to himself. Sweat remembered the radio announcement that cops were in Cadyville. For a split second, his stomach lurched. He and Matt could be in Cadyville at this moment (he was not entirely sure *where* they were). Then again, just because the four wheeler was registered there did not mean this cabin was in Cadyville, Sweat thought. In any event, they had not heard a chopper in some time, so he decided not to worry about it.

He made his way over to Matt, who had remained by the cabin. The front door was locked but one of the windows higher up appeared to be ajar. Matt brought a bucket from the yard and turned it over for Sweat to use as a step. He ascended the makeshift ladder and, lifting the window sill, crawled through before letting Matt in the front door.

A large flat screen television hung on the wall. Several bunks, two sofas, and a small dining table with four chairs filled the space. On the table was a map that appeared to plot the location of two crops on the property. On one of the beds were a few tote bags packed with clothes and blankets. He left most of the clothing (they already had what they needed) except for a hat with the word "Grady's" embroidered on the front, which he had taken from a large plastic bin. As he searched the one-room cabin, adding batteries and bug repellant to his stash, he also found a camo pack. Sweat opened it to find that it contained two items: socks and a black powder pistol. He removed the firearm (having one might invite unnecessary trouble) and handed the pack to Matt, who was noshing on a pickled sausage in between swigs of Southern Comfort. (In Clinton he mostly drank homemade hooch distilled by the inmate Wild Bill. A proper bottle of amber whiskey was therefore a welcome treat.)

On a small stand in front of the television were black and white photographs taken from a trail cam.[27] The pictures unnerved Matt; he did not like the idea of a camera capturing footage of either of them. He went outside and searched for the device, which did not take long; a tree facing directly toward the front house was the only place where a camera could capture the front door from the angle he had seen in the photos. He walked toward the tree and spotted the device strapped to the trunk. Matt pulled it out of its place and brought it back in the cabin to show to Sweat.

"This is where the photos came from," he said, holding up the camera.

---

27 "Trail cams" or trail cameras are used by hunters to track game. (In the Adirondacks, this includes deer and bears.) The devices, many of them camo-colored, are motion activated and are often placed in wooded areas where they record still images and/or video of passing wildlife. Information from these images helps hunters determine best location and time of day to capture game.

Sweat gave it a glance, then shrugged.

"Let's put it back."

Matt threw him a puzzled look.

"What if it took pictures of us?" he asked.

"Well, is it working?"

Upon closer inspection, Matt could see the camera was not turned on.

"No, I don't think so."

"It probably didn't get any pictures of us then."

"Yeah," said Matt, but he removed its SIM card before returning it to the tree, just to be sure.[28]

By the time Matt had put the trail cam back in its proper place, Sweat was ready to pack up and head out. It was a Saturday, and even though it was the off-season for hunting, people in these parts would probably use the weekend to check on their lodges.[29] (Sweat suspected they weren't the kind of people who would be deterred by a prison escape.) Later he and Matt might be able to return to the cabin, and if the coast was clear, they could stay the night and maybe even crank up the generator to watch the evening news.

---

28 Like cell phones, some trail cams also use SIM cards, which allow for these devices to connect to a cellular network. This type of trail cam—also known as a cellular game camera—can send data (i.e. images and video) to a cell phone. Without the SIM card, the camera cannot communicate with a cellular network.

29 In the Adirondacks, early bear season commences on the first Saturday after the second Monday in September. Bow season for deer begins September 27 and continues through the second to last Saturday in October, or the Friday immediately preceding the regular season. This is followed by seven days of muzzleloading—hunting with firearms loaded through the muzzle—before the regular season begins. The summer is considered the off-season.

But the hum of an engine from down the road inter-rupted his thoughts, and runied any chance that they would return that night.

"Matt! Someone's coming!"

Grabbing their bags, they ran outside and ducked behind some brush, in the shadow of a few trees. Within seconds, a truck pulled up and parked in the drive.

An elderly man got out first. He looked from side to side, then toward the cabin door. His eyes narrowed as they roved over the camp. What he saw—or sensed, as there was nothing visibly out of place—caused his lips to purse, then twist into a grimace. He leaned inside the vehicle and grabbed his pump-action shotgun.

Firearm in tow, he made his way to the tree in front of the cabin. He looked around for a moment, then reached for the trail cam. Holding the device, he pressed a small button to dislodge the memory card. Nothing came out.

He looked back at his companions, a middle-aged man and a woman who appeared to be the younger man's girlfriend.

"Someone took the chip," he said.

"C'mon," said the younger. He knew what the elder was implying. "No one's been here."

The latter shook his head.

"I'm telling ya, someone's been here." He surveyed the ground for signs of an intruder and what he noticed made his face turn white: the wet blades of grass at the base of the tree had flattened under the weight of Matt's boot. Someone had, in fact, taken the memory card.

"See there!" he said, pointing at the footprint. "Someone's been here!"

Matt made a motion to stand.

"Stay put!" Sweat hissed. "Don't move a muscle!"

To put the old man at ease—he had quickly dropped his tough-guy exterior—the other man hopped on one of the four wheelers parked on the property and started the engine. He drove up a hill and rode for a few minutes before returning to the cabin.

"Nah, we're good. Nothin' been touched."

The old man gripped his shotgun with firm resolve. His feet stayed planted as if rooted to the ground.

"I'm stayin'."

"C'mon, there ain't nobody here," the younger repeated as he made his way back toward the truck, got in, and turned the ignition. When it was clear to the old man that he would be left behind, he followed, cursing as he went.

When the truck was out of sight, Matt and Sweat sprinted toward the woods. Once they were far enough away, they stopped to catch their breath.

"Do you think they're gonna call the cops?" Matt asked, panting.

Sweat laughed. He thought of the map of crops, the fertilizer, and even the trail cam. By this time, he had put two and two together.

"Bro, they're not going to call the cops. They're pot growers."

DAY NINE

Gov. Andrew Cuomo stood before a small crowd at Yonkers City Hall Sunday in Yonkers, New York, where he had just unveiled a comprehensive $100 million plan to fund schools in the state's neediest districts. Yet when it came time for him to take questions on this topic, reporters were quick to change the subject and ask about the one big story still making headlines.

"On the manhunt part of the operation," said the governor, who appeared to be prepared for such inquiries from the press, "literally, the state police gather tips and leads and you follow up on every lead. And they've had hundreds of leads. We had a lead that [Matt and Sweat] were headed to the state of Vermont, [so] I called the governor of Vermont and we worked out a cooperative agreement with Vermont.[30] We then received information that they

---

30 Law enforcement had reason to investigate whether the fugitives had traveled approximately 20 miles east of Dannemora toward

might just be a few miles from the prison because there was a house that was broken into, and it was suspect, so we followed up on that. Yesterday we had over eight hundred people searching quadrants in an area where we had a tip that they might be.

"The truth is that is the nature of the business. You follow up every tip, you follow up every lead, you are as conscientious as you can be on every lead because you never know which one is going to be the one. We don't know if they're still in the immediate area or if they are in Mexico by now. Enough time has transpired. But we're following up every lead the best we can.

"Second, to the extent that any state employee was involved in facilitating the escape—that is a crime in and of itself and that will be fully prosecuted as a crime in and of itself. We will have zero tolerance for that. I understand prisons run on a delicate balance and having a good relationship between guards and the inmates, guards and the employees, employees and inmates is important. But there's a line and when the line is stepped over, then action has to be taken."

• • •

Corrections Officer Gene Palmer had been proud to work as a Clinton guard. More than twenty-seven years of walking through its locked doors and sliding gates had,

---

Lake Champlain, a large body of water in the northeast corner of New York State. There they might have commandeered a boat and sailed across the lake to Vermont, which also borders this body of water. This turned out not to be the case.

however, taken its toll. His hair, full and red when he first arrived at the facility, had now all but fallen out, and his face was lined from the stress of working in a place with a reputation for violence. The fifty-seven-year-old CO had become admittedly hardened by what he had seen behind the whitewashed perimeter wall. Long-term exposure to knife fights among the inmates and other acts of aggression had, to a degree, desensitized him to brutality—though he still had a level of compassion for those men who ended up in Dannemora. He knew that many of them—a mixture of various races, religions, and upbringings—had come from broken homes. He understood some were mistreated as children. He placed confidence in the prison programs aimed at rehabilitation and supported the inmates' ability to work. Not that Palmer had a bleeding heart. He simply believed in the system.

Throughout his tenure, the CO had become friendly with a few prisoners. For the sake of getting through the day, Palmer treated the inmates more or less the same. At least up until they gave him trouble. Then, as some would later say, all bets were off.

For the last eight years, Palmer had escorted inmates to and from the industry building. The position had put him in close proximity to Richard Matt, and a camaraderie based on mutual gain took shape. Palmer had a distinct distaste for gangs and relied on the "rat system," an informant scheme between prisoners and COs, to gather information about warring groups in the North Yard. The currency would vary—a painting for more art supplies, a television for intel on potential riots—but the overall effect was the same: such transactions, no matter how seemingly benign, fed into the prison's culture of corruption. Any friend of Matt's was safe, several with inside knowledge have said, and any enemy would end up on Palmer's shit list. (And vice versa, as Matt had vowed to kill anyone who wronged the CO.) Inmates worked to stay in Palmer's good graces, and to some, the tall guard with broad, muscular shoulders and a gray goatee held rock star status (a fitting description for the guard, who sang and played lead guitar in the four-member band Just Us, which often took up gigs at Fuzzy Ducks in Morrisonville, New York, performing covers like "Folsom Prison Blues" by Johnny Cash). At times, he was chummy with the men. (The CO often made trips to the tailor shops, where he brought photographs from his latest fishing trip, boasting about the size of the catch.) Yet others had seen a different side of him. As one former inmate put it, Palmer could "flip like a light switch."

Like many of the guards, he had one main goal: get on well with the inmates. The problem was that such equanimity came at a high price.

• • •

Sweat woke at dawn. His stomach growled so he reached in his pack for a granola bar to hold him over. He thought back to the day before, still laughing about the old man with the bolt-action rifle. ("He was like a super badass ready to get down to business!" they had said to each other. "[Then] all the badass went right out of him!") Reliving the encounter kept their spirits up as they hiked along another dirt trail, which led them to a small clearing. Here they came across another deer blind, this one built on scaffolding that stood about twenty feet off the ground, which could be accessed by an accompanying ladder. (At first they passed the shelter and continued west down the mountain to a moss-covered bog, one of the most beautiful displays of vegetation Sweat had ever seen. But, as there was no easy way around the marshland and the sun would soon set, they went back to the deer blind to spend the night.)

The blind had been a good find. It was a sound structure with sliding windows, two sturdy chairs, a built-in table, carpeted floors, and room to stand upright. Here they had slept well enough. Matt, who had woken up for a quick bite, had again drifted off. Now wide awake, Sweat turned the knob of his radio and tuned into the news, where a few voices were discussing the escape. They seemed to be searching for things to say, Sweat thought. There were no real updates so the broadcasters simply reiterated the known facts: law enforcement was still scanning the area, following up on tips, and offering rewards for information that led to their capture. "They're probably soaking wet, cold, miserable, wishing they was back in a warm prison cell with free food," said one voice on the other end of the frequency. The comment made Sweat smile. "Shit," he thought. "I couldn't be much more content if I wanted to be."

And his contentment was even greater this morning: it was his 35th birthday, the first one he had spent free in nearly thirteen years.

He turned off the radio and looked out into the wilderness. Being twenty-some feet in the air he could see quite far; the view was a spectacular sea of green. But a swish in the brush below drew his gaze down to the foot of the blind. Through the leaves he spotted a large black bear foraging in the field. Then, a few moments later, a second bear appeared, this one slightly more brown than its companion. This beast swayed this way, then that, before rising up on its hind legs, its nose wiggling as it sniffed the summer air.

Sweat glanced over at Matt huddled in the corner. He considered waking him but then thought better of it; Matt was not a man of the wild. This would be a moment for him alone, a way to celebrate the day and to look toward the future, to many years in Mexico or somewhere just as far from Little Siberia.

"Damn," he thought as the bears walked back into the forest. "I wish I brought a camera."

BINGHAMTON, NEW YORK—1989

David ran out to the white 1979 Dodge truck that was pulling up outside of his mid-century, multi-family home on Baxter Street. His Uncle Jimmy and his mother's current flame Jerry Edwards—one of her high school sweethearts—had just returned from one of Binghamton's pawnshops with a gift for his ninth birthday: a white bike with brown and orange off-road tires, his very first set of wheels. David gave little thought to the present being used; nearly everything he owned had been previously owned by someone else, even his prized wood-paneled Atari 2600 console and its games, Asteroids and Pong.

He had not yet taken his present for a spin when an unfamiliar red Ford Ranger parked behind Jimmy's pick-up. A gnome-like figure no more than five-feet six-inches tall with a pale complexion and fiery beard climbed out. The man shook his uncle's hand and asked for Pamela. Jimmy pointed up at the house. The man nodded and made his way toward the door.

The boy looked at his uncle. "You'd better go up there," Jimmy said.

David climbed the stairs to their top-floor unit. The stranger stood in the doorway to their apartment, talking to his mother. Even to a nine-year-old the man appeared squat; had his round middle been wrapped in a green coat, David thought, he would surely have been mistaken for a leprechaun.

The two adults exchanged a few words before Pamela turned toward her son.

"This is your father," she said.

David took another look at the visitor. He had not heard much about Floyd Kenyon over the years; only that he had grown up on a farm and left the family after David turned two. The man bore only a faint resemblance to the boy; their Anglo skin held a similar translucence, and in the event that either would furrow his brow, as both did now, a formless splotch of pink would appear above the bridge of their noses.

Floyd told David to follow him back outside. He led him to the Ranger and opened the window of the cap on the truck's bed. From a pile of reels and rods he pulled out one rusty pole. Floyd took it in his pudgy fingers and handed it to David before climbing into the driver's seat and taking off.

Later that day, David, who frequently fished with his uncle, attempted to cast a line in his living room. But instead of forming an effortless arc, the line barely extended beyond the tip of the pole. He pried open the closed face reel to see a tangled mess of wire. The mechanism inside, it seemed, had long been broken.

DAY TEN

MONDAY, JUNE 15TH

Joyce Mitchell stood before Judge Mark Rogers again in Plattsburgh City Court. She had spent the weekend 160 miles south in Rensselaer County Jail, far away from the ongoing manhunt. Her involvement in the escape was the type of scandalous selling point the press loved to pounce on—and Joyce's role in the "love triangle," as some newspapers and television networks liked to put it, had thrust her into the spotlight. She had earned a few unflattering titles, among them "the Hamburglar" for the tool-laden package of frozen meat, and, the tabloid favorite, "Shaw-skank."[31] Yet such words seemed incongruent with the demure prison seamstress standing in the courthouse. Though her bewildered expression had not changed, the bright green t-shirt and blue jeans she had worn at her first proceeding had been traded in for black and white stripes and a bulletproof

31 This nickname is from the film *The Shawshank Redemption*.

vest. And her attorney had changed, too—Keith Bruno had handed over the case to lawyer Stephen Johnston, who was now at her side.

"I've gone over the charges with Miss Mitchell," Johnston said. "Had time to discuss it with her, and what we're going to do right now, judge, is we're going to waive a preliminary felony hearing."[32]

Judge Rogers nodded.

"The matter will be transferred to county court and your next court date will come from county court," said the judge.

Members of Clinton County Sheriff's Department escorted Joyce out of the building, the television cameras following closely behind.

• • •

Cook and White drove up to the corner of Route 374 and Rand Hill Road, just east of the fixed post that had been established there for more than one week. The sergeants had been called to a possible sighting at this location, where their potential witness now sat in a small sedan off the side of the road.

As they approached the vehicle they saw a squat, middle-aged woman in the passenger seat, flailing her arms as if she was swatting at a swarm of bumble bees.

32 In New York State, a defendant can waive the right to a preliminary hearing. This will result in a case being sent directly to the grand jury. Preliminary hearings are rare in New York State; waiving the right to one is a matter of procedure.

"Oh my God! I just saw them! I just saw them!" she wailed through the open window.

"Oh, really?" said Cook, perhaps a little more gruffly than he intended. Most of the complaints he had looked into that week had come from residents who believed their information might be useful to law enforcement. He sensed that this woman was not one of those people.

"Yeah, right there in the woods!" she wept. "They were running! I know what they wear, I used to make inmate uniforms! I know what they look like! I was so scared I spilled my coffee! I'm going to be sick to my stomach!"

With a sigh, the sergeant began to take notes. Every single grievance, no matter how small or unlikely—even if the credibility of the source was in question—had to be documented, investigated, and ruled out.

Since he had been assigned to the detail, Cook and his partner had responded to more calls than they could count. Earlier that week he and White had received word about an American flag hanging upside down.[33] (The job tied up some 15 squad cars for a good hour before a neighbor told them it had been hanging that way since he could remember.) On another occasion, a man who lived along Chazy Lake Road had reported bullets flying through his backyard. (Upon approaching the house, they saw an older man running toward them, holding a shotgun. "What the heck is this guy doing?" Cook had asked his counterpart. It did not take them long to figure out the man simply wanted to be part of the excitement that had come with

33 While it can be considered an act of political protest, flying the American flag upside down is also an official signal of distress according to the United States Flag Code.

the escape. The barracks would later receive several more "tips" from the gentleman until he was told, in so many words, to stop wasting their time.) And in the coming days the sergeants would experience more of the same. (White would soon speak with a woman who, upon noticing that her canoe had floated to the other side of her backyard pond, believed the inmates might have commandeered the vessel and steered it across. On another day, a call would come in from a trooper who reported suspicious activity at a cabin on Westside Road. Before they knew it, the place was teeming with investigators. Law enforcement quickly learned an elderly man lived at the lodge and, since no one had seen him in some time, believed that he was inside being held hostage. The State Police set up a perimeter and brought in a SORT team.[34] "Come out!" they called over the loudspeakers of their Chevy Tahoes. "If you're in there, turn the light on! Answer your phone!" For hours they waited in the pouring rain for a response. Frustrated and soaked, Cook pulled one of the SORT guys aside. "Hey, are you in charge?!" he asked. "Can you guys go in? Find out if he's in there or not?" "Oh no, no," the other said. "We need to send a robot in first before we ever go in."[35] And so it went, until they finally got a hold of the man's daughter,

---

34 SORT or "Special Operations Response Team" is a tactical response unit inside a law enforcement agency. Here it refers to the unit within the New York State Police.

35 During a hostage situation, law enforcement agencies will often send a robot into the dwelling so as to prevent harm to its officers. During the manhunt there were only a handful of these devices at the disposal of the State Police and, as in this case, they would have to wait for one to be brought to the dwelling in question. Such requests were often delayed due to poor reception and proximity of the robot to the desired location.

who explained that her father was hard of hearing and most likely in bed asleep.)

A similar pattern of protocol was applied now near the corner of Route 374. A canine unit was brought in, a perimeter was established, and for more than an hour a team of troopers searched the surrounding woods. B.C.I. investigators later interviewed the woman at her home before determining that she in fact did not see the inmates.

Dead ends like these annoyed Cook and his fellow members of law enforcement. Bad tips and false leads had worn away the certitude they first had ten days before at the beginning of the manhunt. Efforts to apprehend the inmates remained as vigilant as ever, but the search had now become a test of wills.

DAY ELEVEN

TUESDAY, JUNE 16TH

It was well into the night when Matt and Sweat approached a small white cabin off the side of Wolf Pond Road. During its high season, this fifteen-mile stretch connecting the hamlet of Standish (one town west of Dannemora) to neighboring Mountain View is full of hunters who visit the lodges along its boulder-strewn route. In the summer, however, these abodes are all but abandoned. Sweat knew their dwindling stock of granola bars, peanuts, and pepperoni sticks would not last, and hoped that at least one place here would have provisions.

Matt leaned into the dark to open the cabin's front door.

"Locked," he whispered.

Sweat nodded, then went up a set of stairs on the side of the house to try its other entrance. Pulling out his knife, he slipped the blade in the jamb and gently pushed. The door popped open.

He surveyed the room, which looked more or less

like the other clubhouses they had been to so far, with the exception that here, large footlockers had been placed at the end of several of its bunks. Sweat rummaged through the trunks for a few minutes before finding an Army coat. He took the jacket downstairs to show Matt, who, as it turned out, was also inspecting some clothing.

"You should take that," Sweat said of the camo rain gear he was holding. Matt often complained of being cold and wet, and this appeared to be well-made stuff. (Plus, he thought, the pants looked like they would accommodate his friend's midsection.) They collected a few more items—an LED flashlight, packets of grape and raspberry powdered drink mix, some more batteries, and a bowie knife with an Eagle carved into the handle—before locking up.

Farther down the road where Wolf Pond began to curve stood a second cabin. Seeing no signs of life, they tried each of its windows until Sweat found one that was unlocked.

"Here, take my case," he said to Matt, handing the guitar bag over before lifting the sill and squeezing under the metal bars screwed to the outside of the frame. A mattress on the other side caught his landing. He rolled over to take in the surroundings, namely some wall cabinets, a large dresser, bags, bins, boxes, and a few bunks where clothes were hung, ready for when their owners returned.

He walked over to a side door he had seen from the outside and opened it to let Matt in. Yet when he peered out, there was no sign of him.

"Tony!" Sweat yelled. He paused to listen. No answer. "Yo, Tony!"

He looked around. Still, nothing.

"YO, HACKSAW!"

A voice piped up from around the back of the house. "Yeah!" Matt answered.

Sweat walked over to meet him. "You didn't hear me calling you Tony?" he asked as soon as he got close enough.

"Nah, I didn't hear ya."

Sweat laughed. "What's the point of an alias then?" he said, half to himself.

Back inside the lodge—which they learned was called Still Water from a sign tacked to a photo board—were two refrigerators packed with beer. A pad of paper lay on the top of one fridge, where someone had drawn tick marks to keep tally of every can that had been removed.

"Don't take anything," Sweat said.

Matt gave him a sideways look.

"Ok here, take one of those," said Sweat, pointing to the vodka in the back of the bottom shelf.

Matt placed the liquor on a large table in the middle of the space as Sweat began pulling a number of items from the cabinets and countertops (this included black pepper, eight packets of oatmeal, a box of flavored Triscuits, breakfast bars, nutrition bars, and two big cans of baked beans, some Jack Link's sausages, more pepperoni, a can of Mountain Dew, four bottles of water, and a block of jalapeno pepper jack cheese) and a few more things from the bunkroom dresser (among them, one black pair of socks and another wool pair with orange toes).

As they started to pack, Matt marched out of the bedroom wearing a new article of clothing.

"Hey, Dave! Check this out!"

Sweat turned to see him parading around in a gray CO coat.

"Take the jacket off you funny bastard!"

Matt grinned and, still wearing the jacket, walked over to see Sweat leafing through a large journal.

"Hey, what are you doing?" he asked.

"Checking the log book."

Sweat handed over the journal and pointed to the last entry: *"June 14th—Everything looks good. No inmates to shoot."*

Matt's face turned scarlet.

"Let's write them back," he said. "Let's write, 'We were here, you fuckers!'"

"Nah bro, we can't do that."

"Well, let's take this then," said Matt, who had walked over to a corner by the kitchen table where someone had placed a twenty-gauge shotgun.

Sweat frowned.

"We don't need it. They'll know it's missing. People will know where we are."

Matt propped it back up against the wall with reluctance. A firearm would have brought him some peace of mind and a sense of payback, still pissed by what had been written.

It was still dark by the time they left, their packs heavy as they headed out. They walked awhile without event (except for when a plastic part securing the strap of Sweat's pack snapped under the weight of the cargo, which was to be expected, as his was the heavier of their loads) until they came upon another cabin, this one painted in barn red. The single-story lodge bore a front screen door with a white wooden frame, which complemented the white trim of its three barred windows, and Christmas lights—the large, old-school kind—hung from its slanted charcoal roof. A small wooden sign declared this dwelling "The Doll House."

Matt shined his flashlight through one of the windows. The beam fell on a white retro oven against the back wall, several mid-century chairs, a thick round pine table, a bed without sheets, and cooking utensils, which dangled from a small white double door cabinet, along with more pots and pans that hung on the opposite wall, which was made up of teal metal slats, giving the place a rustic, mod feel.

Sweat went to try the front door, where a padlock hung from a sliding barrel bolt above its gold knob.

"Locked up pretty good," he said.

They ventured down Wolf Pond once more, but by 3 a.m. they returned to The Doll House. (They had hiked more than a mile but never came across another cabin. Tired and ready for sleep, they decided to circle back—yet as they walked, howls in the distance gave Matt a start. "Those wolves?" he asked. His voice had gone up an octave. Sweat smiled. "Nah bro. Coyotes.")

Sweat began to search for a way in. He walked toward the side of the cabin, past an open shed with logs stacked to its ceiling, and around the back to the other side, where there was another shed, this one with a wood truss brushed in the same barn red. He squeezed past to reach a narrow window, which thankfully did not have bars. Sweat slipped his knife between frame and sill as he had done before. Knocking out a stick that held it closed, he lifted the sill and slid in.

His flashlight illuminated the space. Several twin-sized beds were pushed up against the walls. A wooden rocking chair with a floral pattern on the back and seat had been pushed to one side. The only real decoration was a red, blue, and white Budweiser poster that hung in between the two front-facing panes of glass.

Sweat moved to the kitchen to let Matt in. He then went over to the retro stove and lit the burner. A blue and gold flame burned brightly underneath. He lowered the oven door and placed their boots there to dry. Seeing that the gas was on (the stove would not have worked without it) he took his pocket lighter and ignited one of the propane lights fixed to the ceiling.

Matt watched the flicker with misgiving.

"Somebody might see that from the road," he said.

"Nobody's going to come down this road this late at night," said Sweat.

He then went toward the bathroom, where he lit another propane light. The glow from above revealed a trap door below his feet. Sweat lifted the door and walked down a ladder into a small cellar where he found two jugs of water and three 12 packs of Mug Root Beer, Sprite, and orange Slice. He brought a couple of sodas for Matt to mix with the vodka his friend had filched earlier that day. More loot—thermal hand warming packs, red glow sticks (of the snap and shake variety), Band-Aids, a small tourniquet, antiseptic, a pair of tweezers, another emergency thermal blanket, and a few bucks and pocket change Matt found was also added to their bounty.

Weary from the hours of walking, they retired for the evening with the understanding that they would leave by dawn.

• • •

BINGHAMTON, NEW YORK—1991

David sat in Broome County Family Court with his mother, his sister Anna, and a social worker. From across the room he could see Floyd Kenyon's flannel shirt and fiery beard. It was the first time he had seen his father in two years. He had thought about him from time to time after his ninth birthday, and, when he did, he wondered why he wasn't around. Maybe, he thought, his father hated him like everyone else did.

The judge said something that David did not hear; he had been too focused on his dad. After court was dismissed, David followed his mother and the lady from social services up the stairs to the parking garage. He saw Floyd a few flights ahead of them and took off running. "Dad!" he called out. "Dad!" The words echoed against the concrete. His mother and the woman yelled after him, but David did not listen.

He caught up to Floyd and threw his eleven-year-old arms around the man's neck.

"Where have you been?" he cried. "Take me with you! I want to go with you, Dad!"

The man looked down at his son, then looked away.

"You can't come with me," he said.

Pamela caught up to them and pulled David in the other direction. Floyd walked to his car, now a beige Ford Escort, and drove off.

It would be the last time he ever saw his father.

DAY TWELVE

Twelve days into the manhunt, the media frenzy that first disrupted Dannemora had fizzled out. Television trucks left the village. Photographers and camera crews packed up their gear. Many out-of-town reporters went home. The journalists had covered the governor's press conferences, the arrest of the prison seamstress, and the unending search—but now, the investigation seemed to be at a standstill. Law enforcement, it appeared, had hit a wall. Tidbits of information had kept the story in the press, but the news was starting to dry up.

In its wake, District Attorney Andrew Wylie took the spotlight.

The small-town prosecutor had become the point person on the escape, making frequent appearances on nearly every television network. At times, as some locals would often say, his remarks felt smarmy and arrogant. Others said he was using the publicity to win him future votes. Some called him vile names, irritated with how he seemed to be capitalizing on the manhunt.

Yet one thing was clear: Wylie had become one of the most accessible officials willing to talk about the prison break. He and his team revealed that Joyce admitted to having sexual relations with Matt, that her subpoenaed cell phone records reflected that she had spoken with Matt's daughter on at least one occasion, and that she had discussed an alleged plot with the inmates regarding the murder of her husband.

With no sign of the fugitives in nearly a fortnight, it was Wylie and his apparent liking of the limelight that moved the story forward.

• • •

Sweat heard the sound of crunching. He followed the noise out of the bathroom to the bunkroom and looked out the window to the shed with the woodpile. A porcupine was gnawing at one of its beams. He tapped on the glass but the critter continued, quite content with its project.

Sweat lifted the window to get a better look.

"Hey!" he called out into the mountain air. "You're making too much noise!"

The creature paused and cocked his head to better see the caller, its pincushion of quills still quivering. "Who the hell are you?" he seemed to say, and promptly returned to his noisy activity.

It was midmorning, and Matt and Sweat had already prepared a few packets of oatmeal and brewed several cups of coffee with a stovetop percolator from some grounds they had found on top of the fridge. They passed the day washing dishes, sweeping the floors, and returning items they had moved the night before to prepare for their evening departure. (While cleaning up they found a photo of a man with an owl on his shoulder; a label said the dude's name was Pickles, and they presumed he owned the cabin.) A few meals later—Triscuits and peanut butter and jelly washed down with vodka and Mountain Dew for lunch, baked beans Matt doused in hot sauce for dinner—they packed up their trash and slipped out the window, leaving The Doll House more or less the way they had found it.

They walked along the road before turning right to follow a truck trail. The path veered left, leading them to another cabin with an attached mobile home. From the photographs on the wall, the place seemed to belong to an older couple with grandchildren. Here, they took only a few items, including one rain poncho, more bottles of water, a few maps, and a black and red hiking pack Matt had found for Sweat, who now stood on the porch moving their belongings to the new bag before walking into the woods to toss the ratty guitar case.

The men took to the road once more—walking under the powerlines, their long limbs towering overhead—until their legs grew tried. They made for a berm, which offered at least a little shelter. Matt pulled out a wad of garbage bags and began to lay them on the damp ground. After drinking some more water, flavored with raspberry powder, they laid down to sleep.

● ● ●

KIRKWOOD, NEW YORK—DECEMBER 1999

Less than six months since he finished his last bid for burglary, nineteen-year-old David brought his bowling ball to Sunset Lanes in Kirkwood, twelve miles southeast from his home in Binghamton. A few friends gathered around the table where Sweat set up; among them was Heather, the attractive teen he fooled around with in the back of his car. Heather knew she and Sweat weren't serious, and, at least at this juncture, they were on the same page when it came to romance.

Sweat lifted his ball, a green and blue marbled beauty with "Dave" engraved on its smooth surface. The weight of the globe felt more like a feather in his hand, and he used his substantial young muscle and the ball's heft to his tactical advantage. David never put a fancy spin on his throw; that wasn't his style. All he ever needed was focus and speed.

He had drawn the ball back and closed in on the center pin when he felt a playful pinch on his ass. He wheeled around to see a smiling April, who would later be the love of his life. April was a girl from Afton, about thirty miles east of where David lived, and part of the teenage crowd that congregated at the lanes. She possessed a shapely figure for sixteen, and her auburn hair, which fell gently at the shoulder and held the sweet aroma of Pantene, accentuated her sensuality.

April's mother—whom David and Heather knew, as all three worked at Flechar Manufacturing Co.—was also at the alley that night. David asked her permission to take April out to a nearby Denny's. Heather tagged along; she and April were good friends, and Heather assured April's mom that she would drive her daughter home after dinner.

After taking their seats at Denny's, April requested another fork since hers was covered in water spots. While they waited for their meal, she took out a book and began to read, ignoring the baffled expressions from across the table. When dinner arrived, April poked at the grilled chicken on top of her salad, declared it undercooked, and sent this back too.

David paid the bill and walked outside to warm up the car. The cold air had caused a small crack in his windshield to spread like a spider web across the glass. April had struck him as odd and unapologetic, which made her all the more attractive.

The girls hopped in the vehicle. David asked if they wanted to come over, hoping to get lucky. They were on to him though, and declined, leaving David's car as quickly as they had entered. Heather took April home, and David spent the night thinking about her.

DAY THIRTEEN

Jeremiah Calkins stood outside the Mobil gas station along Route 9 in the outskirts of Plattsburgh, a complimentary one-way Greyhound ticket in his hand. It was just after daybreak when two corrections officers had plunked him down at this solitary pit stop on the side of the road, a place where newly released inmates were dropped off nearly every morning to catch a bus home, or wherever it was they wanted to go. He was happy to finally be free of Clinton's Annex, the lower security part of the prison that, in recent days, had felt more like a supermax. Conditions there had never been great, particularly compared to the county jails where he had previously been incarcerated. But things had gotten a lot worse in the fortnight since Matt and Sweat had made their getaway.

"This is my first day out," he said to an inquiring journalist that morning, looking up toward the summer sun that shone on the endless rows of cow's corn.

"They've been getting cracked down on by Albany,

and they're taking it out on us," he continued, referring to Clinton's guards. "Their attitude towards us has changed. They'll write us up for just small stuff. They like to put hands on you, on the inmates. Just the other day when we got searched on the block, they took a guy and beat him up over some small thing. He wasn't a young guy; he was an older guy. You could hear the slapping noise. He came back and his side was all banged up. They were screaming at him, calling him real degrading names. They've been doing a lot of stuff like that."

Calkins said he would often pass Matt in the North Yard. His reputation preceded him; Calkins had heard rumors about Matt's escape from Erie County Correctional Facility in the mid-1980s while doing a stint for third-degree assault. It was here, Calkins had been told, that Matt had begun to paint, and would sell the works to COs for profit—though neither the breakout nor the art was ever discussed at length. Gossip had continued to swirl since he and Sweat had crawled their way out of Clinton, the favorite belief being that Matt and Sweat had gifted paintings in exchange for the tools. That part, at least, had pretty much been true.

By 7 a.m., the bus had pulled up to one of the pumps. The driver stepped out to summon the three men waiting to board. Calkins, now a free man after serving one year for third-degree rape, tossed his white cloth drawstring bag over his shoulder before turning back to the journalist.

"[Matt] seemed like an all-right person. But when you're locked up, everybody can be deceiving."

• • •

KIRKWOOD, NEW YORK—2001

David and April moved into a modest two-bedroom apartment on Roberts Street in Kirkwood, just across from his mother Pamela's place and a five-minute drive from Felchar Manufacturing Co., where April had also taken a job after graduating from high school. They had paired off within the year after meeting in Sunset Lanes and had soon become inseparable. Weekends were reserved for road trips to the docks of Cayuga Lake, and evenings were spent at Friendly's restaurant splitting Reese's Peanut Butter Cup Sundaes. During that summer, they could be seen running around their backyard with Tasha, a rescue Rottweiler pup David's boss had given them, or out with other couples like Dennis and Christine. David would often come home to the sweet smell of chocolate chip cookies, and April, entering an empty apartment, would find small signs of his affection. (He loved to set April's Reba McEntire CD to her favorite song and leave a note to "hit play.") And most nights, they made love—the young, hungry, unapologetic kind of sex that knew no restraint.

By early 2001, April was pregnant. Friends congratulated them. Family members from her side surprised them with a baby shower. Co-workers at Felchar's shared in their joy, though many were disappointed when David resigned because of complications with April's pregnancy. Emergency hospital visits became more frequent as the due date approached. They moved in with David's cousin, Jeff Nabinger, who lived on Dickinson Street in Binghamton, a temporary solution to their lack of income.

Then, on October 27, the day finally came.

"My water just broke," said April, *standing in the doorway near their bedroom.*

David looked around.

"Really? O.K., let's get to the hospital."

He rushed out to their Honda Prelude, slid the key into the ignition, and turned. The engine clicked and sputtered but would not start.

"Oh, c'mon!" he said to himself.

David ran over to their neighbor's place. He told the man his girlfriend was about to give birth and he needed a jump. They hooked up the cars, re-booted the battery, and within minutes, he and April were on their way to Our Lady of Lourdes Hospital.

They called their mothers, who arrived soon after. Other relatives also began to show up. After hours of contractions, April could tell it was time. The nurse shooed everyone out except for David, who stood with the doctor near the end of the bed.

April pushed. David could see the top of the baby's head.

"I love you," she said. Her face was clammy and smooth with youth and calm. She made the whole thing look easy, he thought.

David smiled. "I love you." He never responded with "too;" to him, this word implied an obligatory response. He had said these words not because she said them first, but because he meant them with everything he had.

Then their son was born.

"Who wants to hold him?" asked the nurse, cradling the child.

"Me!" said David, grinning. "She got to hold him for nine months!"

They laughed as he stretched out his arms to take the baby boy, whom they named Bradly. David chose the name, which he took from a character in Home Improvement—Bradly was the eldest boy on the family sitcom, known for his athleticism and proficiency with mechanical work. When he was older, David thought, they could call him Brad. It was a strong name, just what he wanted for his first-born son.

He looked down at the infant. He had his mother's eyes, although his were more blue than the bright green of April's. Even his brow and cheekbones seemed to be hers. But there was also something in the baby's face, something he could not quite pinpoint, that had come from his father.

David beamed.

"I have everything I could ever want."

DAY FOURTEEN

FRIDAY, JUNE 19TH

By Friday morning, the U.S. Marshals had added the escapees to its 15 Most Wanted fugitives list. One hundred and sixty-eight state troopers from the New York State Police had been assigned to a 24-hour roving patrol. Dozens of investigators continued to pursue new leads. Age progression mug shots of the inmates had been released. Search parties had cleared more than six hundred miles of trails through Clinton and Franklin Counties, where abandoned buildings, seasonal camps, railroad beds, and hundreds of occupied homes had been investigated, yet no sign of the inmates had surfaced.

"We're not going anywhere," said Guess, speaking at an 11 a.m. press conference outside of Clinton. "Our plan is to pursue these men relentlessly and until they are in custody. We will not stop our search and we will not stop chasing leads until we have put Richard Matt and David Sweat back in prison."

• • •

"Here, take these."

Sweat pushed a pile of cigarette butts toward Matt, then handed him a wad of rolling papers. He had spent the afternoon scouring the cabin for the discarded ends. Even a few grams of tobacco might diminish the side effects of Matt's nicotine withdrawal, he thought, and therefore curb his desire to hit the bottle.

Matt's mouth widened in a goofy, inebriated grin.

"Where'd you get these? I looked all over the place!"

Sweat laughed. It was clear his friend's vision had been compromised by the spirits.

"Hey, what's that?" Matt's eyes roved from the ends and fell on the fifty-cent piece Sweat was flipping in his hand.

Sweat held it up for him to see.

"Nah," Matt said. "I've got something better for you."

He reached into his pocket and pulled out a silver dollar. Sweat eyed it with interest; it must have come from the box of coins tucked away in a hole in the ceiling that he had come across earlier that day.

"Why are you keeping all of the change?" he asked. "It's just added weight."

"It's still money and I'm going to buy you a Pepsi out of a soda machine with it! You wait and see."

Sweat grinned. In that moment, his friend reminded him of the man who sings the melody of "Midnight Rider": a guy on the run with nothing more to his name than a silver dollar.

"A Pepsi!? Just want what I've always wanted."

The last twelve hours had been normal, as life on the

road went. They had begun with a morning wash in a nearby creek, where they had also collected water to boil for their breakfast (oatmeal and coffee), lunch (baked beans and macaroni elbows with fried pepperoni, hot sauce, and seasoning), and dinner (more macaroni elbows). A few notable things differentiated this day from the rest: Matt had fallen through the floorboards of the back deck, which were all but rotted out. He had also discovered a twenty-gauge shotgun under one of the mattresses. (Sweat had found it first and had hoped Matt would not see it. There was not much he could do, Sweat thought, other than to let him have it.) But on the whole, the day was more or less uneventful—just how they wanted it to be.

Rain now tapped on the roof of Twisted Horn (Sweat would later find out the cabin's name). As the day waned, he rolled a joint with some weed he had found, and poured himself a glass of black cherry moonshine. Across from him, Matt twirled his recently claimed Bowie knife between his fingers.

He held up the blade, brandishing the eagle on its handle for Sweat to see.

"You know who gave me this?" he asked. "My friend gave me this."

Sweat smiled. He knew Matt was sloshed, but the remark meant something to him all the same. As they smoked and drank, he thought back to something he heard that morning on his transistor radio. A DJ announced that he would dedicate a song to the escapees. A moment later Paul McCartney began to croon to "Band on the Run" as members of the Wings strummed in the background.

DAY FIFTEEN

SATURDAY, JUNE 20TH

John Stockwell secured his blue Yamaha four wheeler in the bed of his white GMC truck, slammed the tailgate shut, and climbed into the driver's seat next to his dog, Dolly. It had been more than a month since the forty-seven-year-old CO and his six-year-old black Labrador retriever had visited Twisted Horn. Weeks of rain and long shifts at Upstate Correctional Facility in Malone had kept him from the cabin since May 2, and it was high time to check the trail cams. Stockwell had hoped to see a big buck or maybe even a moose passing through the property. (He had previously captured these beasts on film and proudly hung the black and white prints on the wall of his wooden shed. "Trail cams have added honesty and integrity to the hunting experience," Stockwell once said. "If you got two bucks on camera and someone says, "Ah, no ya don't!" it's proof you're not lying!")

He had allotted three hours for the trip—enough

time to drive to Wolf Pond Road, unload the ATV, ride three-quarters of a mile into camp and walk another half a mile to the trail cams before returning to his home in Lyon Mountain. Stockwell—a kind-faced man with a ruddy complexion and a build that suited his name—expected to be back by early afternoon. He had promised his wife, Nancy, that they would pick berries in their garden, then head into town for a twenty-eighth anniversary dinner at Donovan's restaurant. The joint would surely be buzzing with chatter about Dannemora, Stockwell thought. Some locals were sure the prisoners were long gone ("They're in Mexico by now, make no mistake!" they would often say), although Nancy was not convinced. Before her husband walked out the door that morning, she asked that he take two items with him: her cell phone and his .38 Smith & Wesson. Stockwell had never been one to have a mobile, and he never brought a firearm to Twisted Horn in the off-season, let alone his handgun. Yet he could see his wife was worried about his journey into the woods, and he readily obliged. "An extra precaution," he said to himself as he holstered the weapon. "Just in case."

Within an hour, Stockwell was parked off to the side of Wolf Pond Road. Days of unrelenting deluge had softened the earth, and the normally hardpan ground sunk beneath his feet. He unloaded his quad (even his pickup could not handle the rough path to the cabin) and scanned the forest floor. Seeing no tire tracks, paw prints, or footsteps, he proceeded with Dolly up ahead, poking her nose in balsam spruces and bounding through mud holes along the way.

Twenty minutes later, Stockwell rounded the corner to Twisted Horn, which he shared with a few other buddies who had also inherited the place. The lodge was not much to look at from the outside; sheets of metal had been bolted to its walls and the roof of its attached shed—a hodge-podge of nailed planks, boards, and other materials—slanted in a precarious way, weighed down in part by vegetation that had sprouted on its surface. Yet the place offered a cozy refuge in the woods. It was theirs, and to Stockwell, that's really all that mattered.

The CO could just make out the cabin when he noticed that Dolly had stopped short, her ears pointed at attention, her eyes on the door. She did not move.

Stockwell pulled the quad closer.

"What the hell is she doing?" he thought.

Then, through the dingy glass window of the bunk-house, he saw it: the back of a head and the top of a shoulder.

He hit the brakes twenty feet from the door.

"Holy fuck, somebody's in there!" he thought.

Stockwell pulled out his revolver and pointed it at the cabin. He turned off the ignition.

"Who are you?!" he hollered. "You better fucking come out!"

• • •

Four empty liquor bottles lay strewn on the floor of Twisted Horn. The twenty-ounce bottle of vodka-Mountain Dew mix Matt had brought from The Doll House had also been drained. All that was left was a bit of the cherry moonshine.

Sweat wanted to leave as early as possible, as weekend mornings meant it was more likely that someone would stop by. They had already washed up and eaten; now all that was left to do was to clean, pack, and bury their garbage out back.

Yet Matt was moving slowly. As he drank the last remaining drops of homemade whisky, Sweat coaxed him to speed up. But Matt, groggy and bleary-eyed from the booze, wanted to linger there a little longer.

Just then, a rumble came from down by the road. Sweat darted to the front door and cracked it open to listen. From a distance he could see a black dog, followed closely by a four wheeler.

"Someone's coming!" he shouted. "Let's go!"

• • •

"Don't go running in there, John," Stockwell thought to himself. "You stay right where you are. Whoever this is you make them come out. Make them show themselves."

The CO sat on the ATV, his .38 caliber still raised. His firearm training had taught him one crucial thing: never lower your weapon.

Another flash of movement. Through the slats in the shed, Stockwell could see that someone had run across his back deck.

"Stay where you are!" he hollered. His grisly, deep voice carried across the property. "You better fucking come out! Who are you? *Who are you?!*"

His black Lab began to pace, her fur standing on end, her eyes fixed on the camp.

"*Stay! Stay, Dolly! Easy! Stay!*"

A deafening crack came from around the back. The

noise brought Dolly to a halt. A second person had run across the deck.

Stockwell's temples beat with blood.

"If you don't come out and start saying something, the next movement I see you're getting it. I'll shoot ya."

Dolly bared her teeth.

"Easy, Dolly!"

Then a loud bang came from somewhere behind the cabin, followed by the sound of splashing water.

Stockwell immediately knew whoever was in Twisted Horn had gone out the back and slid down the steep embankment into the creek.

"OK, John," he told himself. "Time to get the fuck out of here."

He got on the quad and started up the engine.

"Come! *Come,* Dolly! *Let's go!"*

Stockwell drove down the path as fast as the terrain would allow, Dolly at his heels.

• • •

Sweat could still hear the man's words as he skidded down the embankment: "Who's in there?! Come out of there! *Who are you?!"* He had grabbed his bag and old boots and bolted out the back door. Matt ran right after him, skating down the hill. They sprinted some thirty yards to the creek. Sweat tossed his boots in the water.

"Don't matter now," Sweat thought as he discarded the shoes. "They already know we're here." There was no cell service this deep in the woods. He just hoped it would buy them time.

Matt caught up. He appeared more lucid than he had been at Twisted Horn. The sprint seemed to have sobered him up.

"Can you zip up my bag?"

Sweat nodded and went to secure the pack when he noticed it was almost empty.

"Where the hell's all your stuff?!"

"It fell out in the creek."

Sweat groaned. He was glad he had enough provisions for the two of them.

"How the hell did you do that?"

"My bottle was sticking out the top. Caught a branch."

Sweat looked back at his friend. He had grown weary of instructing him every step of the way. But he decided to leave it be. The troopers would not be far behind.

"C'mon," he said. "We've got to get moving."

• • •

Stockwell's own thoughts had taken him aback. He was so close—*so very close*—to firing his weapon. He had never wanted to shoot another human being before, yet there he had been, ready to pull the trigger. He had been pretty sure who those people were. At the very least, he was damn near positive they weren't locals.

"If this was [just] some kid out there banging his girlfriend, stealing the booze, he's going to be out front begging for mercy," he had said to himself as he made his way back to the truck. "Whoever they were, them two motherfuckers knew this ol' redneck wasn't playing games."

Part way down the trail, Stockwell hit the brakes of his

quad. He suddenly remembered Nancy's cell. He pulled it out and dialed 911.

The mobile began to ring.

"Hello? *Hello!?*" he said before someone even picked up the receiver. "This is John Stockwell! I'm at my camp! I just ran into two people!"

The call did not go through.

"Damn signal," he thought.

Ten minutes later he had reached his truck. He jumped off the four wheeler, removed the key, and left the bike parked on the side of the trail. He could not be bothered with loading up it up now.

Dolly jumped into the front seat. Stockwell started the engine and hit the gas.

Not a moment later he heard the second deafening sound of the day.

Clang! Clang! Clang!

Stockwell gave a start.

"*What the hell?*"

He stopped and got out of the truck to see that the ATV ramp was still attached to the tailgate, dragging noisily. In his haste, he had forgotten to unhook it from the vehicle. He quickly undid the straps and threw it to the side.

"*Don't have time for this!*" he thought. He had settled on the idea that the people in his cabin were the fugitives, and each minute that went by meant they would be that much farther away.

Stockwell drove along Wolf Pond Road and made for the local bar and restaurant Belly's to call the authorities. The cell was useless; he needed a landline.

Halfway there he saw about ten quads parked off to the side. He pulled up and rolled down the window.

"I just came from my camp, and there's people up there that shouldn't be there, and they took off running through the woods!" His words collided into one another as he struggled to catch his breath. "I'm not fucking kidding! Get a hold of 911!"

A young man on one of the bikes spoke up first.

"Trooper cars just went down the road here. You just missed them! I'll go find them!"

With that the young man took off.

Stockwell started to drive again when he heard a voice come out of Nancy's cell, still clenched in his hand.

"911," it said. "What is your emergency?"

• • •

"That's how we're crossing."

Sweat pointed to a large fallen tree, spanning the width of a river some twenty-five feet across and fairly deep by the looks of it. Back at the CO's cabin, a map on the wall had indicated that to keep traveling west, they would have to hit a road on the other side of this body of water. Swamps bordered either side of where they stood; to go around would've taken them days. They did not have that kind of time.

Matt eyed the tree with suspicion.

"Are you serious?"

The question annoyed Sweat. "Can you see another way? Look, I'll go first."

Gripping the bark with his feet, Sweat edged his way

over until the limbs of a smaller tree were within reach. He grabbed one of the thicker ones and swung to the other side.

Sweat smiled, pleased with his dexterity. "*Just like Tarzan,*" he said to himself.

He called back to Matt.

"C'mon, Tony!" He laughed, still determined to use his friend's alias.

Matt sighed and began to inch his way over. Not more than a minute later the branch started to bow under his weight. A concerned look spread across his face.

"It's alive, it can take a bit of bend," said Sweat. He tried to sound reassuring. "Here, toss me your gun."

Matt threw the firearm to him, then quickly crawled to the other side.

With the search in full swing they would need a place to lie low, Sweat thought. They hiked through the wilderness until they arrived at a brown three-story house shaped like a wedge. After finding that its first-floor doors and windows were locked, Sweat thought to try his luck with those on the second story. He brought a ladder over from a nearby shed and propped it against the window. He was almost at the top when he heard the sound of a vehicle. He looked up to see a state trooper drive by.

Sweat found this window was unlocked ("Good," he thought), and slid himself through. He rushed down the stairs to Matt and let him in. They gave a quick look around, but apart from some black pepper, found little worth taking. A few days ago, they might have stayed. But after the scare at Twisted Horn and with cops casing the joint, Sweat did not wish to linger. After returning the ladder, they made for the woods.

They walked back up along the road, crossed a river, and stopped on the side of a hill. The sound of rushing wind made them wheel around. Another cop car had just flown by.

"Maybe it's a check point or something farther up—"

Matt did not even get the words out before they heard the sound of a vehicle again.

A trooper was coming back their way.

• • •

The sudden voice of the 911 operator nearly sent Stockwell out of his seat.

"Hello? *Hello!?*"

"Yes!" he yelled into the phone. "Can you hear me!?"

When he heard no response, he looked at the screen. The call had dropped again.

Stockwell looked in his review mirror. He could still see the group of ATV riders. One of them was waving him over. He drove back, and the man who had flagged him down handed him a cell.

"I got 911!"

Stockwell took out his driver's license.

"This is who I am," he said to the man on the bike. He was done dealing with mobile phones. He went over the information again: two men had broken into his cabin off Wolf Pond Road. "Tell them I'm driving a white GMC, and I'm going back. My gate's right off the Wolf Pond Road."

Stockwell got back in his truck and wheeled around. There was no need to go to Belly's now.

By the time he arrived at the gate to Twisted Horn, two troopers were already there waiting for him.

• • •

"Ok. That wasn't cool," Sweat said. The cop had slowed his car in front of the brown house before taking off again. "No way he saw us, but I think it's time to head back into the woods."

As they walked they came across one cabin, then another, and another after that, yet most had little to offer. (Sweat found an ornate glass bottle of Crown Royal in one. He had never tasted the Canadian whisky before and so took a pull. "Tastes overpriced," he thought, and left it. Matt found a blue hoodie in the bunkroom of the same place. Sweat was not thrilled about the bright color, but he knew Matt needed gear. Most of his clean clothes were now floating in the creek behind Twisted Horn.)

The fourth lodge they came across (a contractor's camp, Sweat thought, by the looks of it) was more fruitful, with beef stew, baked beans, cheese, nuts, soda, a pack of gum—it had been more than ten years since Sweat had tasted it—twenty-gauge shells (bird shot mostly), and another (better) ball compass.

As Sweat gathered these things, he turned to see Matt pouring Jack Daniels into a flask.

"Dude, you can't take the flask. They'll notice that it's gone."

"They won't notice."

Sweat held back. He did not want to argue. He had not seen how full the whiskey was to begin with, but he had watched Matt tip the bottle back a few times. Soon, Matt would be drunk again.

The incident at the CO's camp had put Sweat on high alert. He knew the guard had reported their break-in; he had heard it on the radio. They had seen the troopers drive by. The place would soon be flooded with law enforcement. They could not afford another mistake.

• • •

Stockwell could see the state trooper cars parked along Wolf Pond Road. He pulled up and walked over to the first officer he saw: Sgt. Robert Dixon of the New York State Police.

"Hi, sir. I'm wearing a sidearm, here's the permit—"

The sergeant held up his hand.

"No, no, don't worry about that," said Dixon, a tall, muscular man with dark skin who looked younger than his years. His voice was low and grave. "Tell me what happened."

Stockwell took a deep breath.

"Right. There was two people up there that shouldn't have been in that camp. They took off running right down the brook. I called but they wouldn't come out. Make no mistake about it, sir. There was people up there."

Dixon seemed satisfied.

"Ok, bring us to the camp."

Stockwell led them up the road for a mile and a half before Twisted Horn came into view. The sergeant turned to the CO.

"Stay here. If something happens, get out of here."

Stockwell shook his head. "I don't run. I'm going to be right here."

Dixon nodded and moved in with his men. They searched the shed, the wood pile on the opposite side, the bunk room, the living area, and around the shoddy deck, but found no signs of life.

He walked back out to Stockwell.

"You said you didn't go in there, right?"

"That's right."

"OK. I want you to go in and check it out, see if there's anything out of place. Don't touch anything."

Stockwell proceeded through the front door. He looked around the living area. An open box of macaroni elbows sat out in plain view. On the table were towels and a pair of tweezers, as if a minor surgery had been performed. Stockwell's own camo Crocs with faux fur lining had been placed underneath the table. An old percolator, one he had not used in years, still smelled of freshly brewed coffee grounds. His mason jars of moonshine had been emptied. Near the door to the deck was a plastic garbage bag hanging from a screw in the wall.

Stockwell peeked inside and saw a pair of worn out insoles. He turned to Dixon.

"When we leave here in the fall everything's put away, everything's clean," he said. "This garbage ain't ours."

The sergeant came up from behind to look in the bag.

"Uh huh," he said with conviction.

Dixon took out his phone and began to search for a signal.

• • •

Cook's phone rang in his pocket. He pulled over his Crown Vic and flipped open his cell.

"Hello?"

A commander's voice came over the line.

"Where are you? We need you on Wolf Pond Road, they've got a possible sighting. They want your team up here."

"Well, first I heard of it." He had not heard a single transmission come over the radio. "Damn service," he thought.

Thirty minutes later he arrived at the scene. Dozens of squad cars had already swarmed the area, chopper blades whirring overhead.

He looked at the old dirt path that went up into the woods. "Must lead to the camp," he supposed. It appeared to be a long road, at least half a mile from where he stood. He did not want to try and drive any closer for fear of getting blocked in. Instead he joined the other troopers lined up along the side of the road, waiting for their next order.

Night had fallen by the time Cook learned the details of what had happened at Twisted Horn. Word was already beginning to spread that investigators were combing the place for DNA evidence, which they would rush to New York State Police crime lab in Albany.[36] Within thirty-six hours they would have the results of the tested items—a rarity in terms of DNA processing. Determining a match could take up to months or even years in an average crim-

---

36 The New York State Police sends the bulk of its evidence to its Forensic Investigation Center, the Crime Laboratory System Headquarters in Albany, New York, for DNA testing. The center also houses the state's DNA Databank.

inal case due to backlog. With the manhunt came a sense of urgency. A match would be an almost indisputable confirmation that the inmates were now in these parts, and would thus direct their next course of action.

Cook soaked in the excitement. Fifteen days of wading through deluge, chasing hundreds of leads, and vetting each and every possible sighting with little success had worn away the confidence of his men. This sighting awakened the fire Cook felt at the beginning of the search. Now there was hope.

DAY SIXTEEN

Hard rain drops rapped against the siding of the fifth wheel camper where Matt and Sweat had been holed up for 24 hours. After leaving the contractor's camp Saturday, they had walked for quite some time through another downpour in search of a place to spend the night. Matt had fallen behind more than once, due to drink more than to fatigue, yet they finally found their way to the camper parked in a small clearing. Its owners had kept a few items in the place, including a camo rain suit, Band-Aids, super rubber epoxy, black contractor garbage bags, cans of beef stew, Green Mountain Fresh Roast coffee, and a near full bottle of Red Stag.

By mid-afternoon, Matt had consumed more than half of the bourbon. Swaying under its influence, he turned to Sweat.

"If I don't make it, you got to promise me you'll look in after my daughter and make sure she's all right."

Sweat raised his eyebrows. He knew Matt's words were

influenced by the whiskey, though that did not seem to fully explain them. It had been Matt's idea to escape, his idea to bring Joyce on board, his decision to go even when she did not show. "You left me no choice but to grow old and die in here," he had written to the guards. "I had to do something."

"What do you mean if you don't make it?" Sweat asked. "What happened to, 'We're gonna make it, we're gonna make it?'"

Matt appeared small as he sunk further into the cushions of the trailer's slouchy sofa.

"I'm just saying, if I don't, you've got to promise me. And you've got to make it."

"Dude, stop saying you're not going to make it."

"Just promise me."

Sweat breathed a heavy sigh. In six months of preparations and sixteen days on the run, this was the first time Matt had shown signs of surrender.

"If something does happen, I'll do what I can," he said. "But stop saying that shit."

• • •

Sweat woke from a nap to the glug of liquid. He turned over in the chair where he had slept to see Matt draining the last of the Red Stag. The pot of rain water he had collected for them to drink was also gone. He assumed Matt had used it as a chaser.

Sweat was seething but said nothing. "There's no point," he thought. "What's done is done."

The plan was to head out that night, though he could not see how it would work with Matt this hammered.

His boozing, nicotine cravings, and inexperience in the wilderness had slowed them down considerably. The series of mishaps they'd experienced could all be chalked up to Matt's drinking, with the incident at Twisted Horn the most damning of them all.

Sweat knew it would have been easier to continue on alone, but he continued to dismiss the idea. He did not intend to leave his friend behind.

As he considered their next move, Sweat heard Matt mumble something from across the room.

"C'mon, motherfucker, I'm ready to go."

Sweat sat upright.

"Did you just call me a motherfucker?"

Matt had been caught off guard. He thought Sweat was still asleep.

"No."

"Yes you did. I heard you. 'C'mon, motherfucker, I'm ready to go.' If you want to go, go, but I'm not leaving 'til dark. I'm not going to get caught or killed because you want to drink. I'll go my own fucking way first."

"Well if you feel that way, then you should just shoot me in the head."

Sweat's eyes widened. Whatever he had expected Matt to say, this wasn't it.

"What the fuck are you talking about!? You're fucking drunk."

"No, I'm not."

"The fuck you aren't."

Matt's face relaxed. His eyes dropped to the floor.

"Well, maybe I am."

They both fell silent.

• • •

The fifth wheel camper faded into the backdrop as they made for the road, barely visible now that the pale moon was high. Sweat had hesitated to leave with Matt this drunk, but they were low on food. They had no choice but to press on through the downpour.

The men trudged through the rain until lights coming up from behind gave Sweat a start.

"Let's get off the road," he said, pulling Matt to the side.

Sweat scanned the ground for a trail, wiping the rain from his brow. The two men hunched their backs against the deafening torrent and plodded through the muck until they found a path that led to a small gated cabin.

They had just begun to search for a way in when the hum of an approaching engine stopped them mid-step. A police truck sped past, its rubber wheels whooshing through the rushing water.

They stood still to listen, then heard a second vehicle go by.

"C'mon, we gotta get in!" Matt shouted over the gale.

"What do you think I'm trying to do!?" Now was not the time to be sloppy, Sweat thought. Cops knew they were in these parts. They would be checking the cabins. Another mistake could do them in.

Not a second later he heard glass shatter on the other side of the cabin. He tore around the corner to see that Matt had broken a porch window while trying to force its lock.

"What the fuck, dude?!" This would be a clear sign

of break-in. "Find a branch and stick in the window so it looks like the storm did it!"

"What a waste," Sweat thought. They could not stay here, not after this.

With no sign of the trooper vehicles, the men proceeded down the road once more. By then the rain had stopped, and a balmy mist hung low in the air. Sweat began to strip off his outer layers; the heat trapped in his jacket felt stifling. For several miles he led them with Rambo-like stealth, as one unsteady step might sound the alarm.

As before, the glow of headlights brought them to a halt. At first, their presence seemed benign; the beams had shown just over a hill in the distance, far from the way they had come. Yet after they rounded a corner, the headlights seemed to move faster. Before they knew it, the lights were approaching them with increased speed.

Sweat dashed off the road toward the forest. The slick ground caused him to slip and slam his knee into a boulder, sending him airborne. He flipped over into a ditch, his tailbone jamming into the small of his back.

Matt sprinted over and crouched beside him.

"You OK!?"

"Yeah," Sweat said. His voice wheezed from getting the wind knocked out of him.

Matt nodded then pointed toward the road. "I see a flashlight."

The headlights had belonged to a state trooper, who now stepped out of the vehicle. He directed his beam toward the muddied ground, illuminating the path they had walked only moments before.

"Shit," Sweat whispered, rubbing his aching knee. "He's following our footprints."

The unexpected click of Matt's shotgun hammer gave Sweat a start.

"Dude, you can't shoot that cop! If you shoot that cop, they'll know where we are and kill us. We'll head down the hill."

Matt snapped the hammer back in place. He had grown tired of taking orders.

"Fine," he said. "I'll lead."

BINGHAMTON, NEW YORK—JULY 3, 2002

Shawn Devaul waited near the corner of Mulbery and Chenago Streets in Binghamton, scanning the roads. A company work stoppage had recently forced him out of a manufacturing gig at Southern Tier Plastics. Crime had never appealed to the tall, lanky twenty-three-year-old, at least never enough for him to take part in a plan like this. But unemployment and the birth of his baby girl had made him desperate. His daughter and her mother lived out in Greene, about twenty-five miles north, and Shawn needed cash—more than one lousy check's worth—to move the family under one roof. He had been relying on someone else to get him to Greene, namely David Sweat (better known as Dave), the guy in his circle of Binghamton friends who had a car.

They found themselves increasingly in one another's company in the weeks of the summer of 2002, before their lives were forever changed by a series of fatal decisions—before, as Shawn put it, "everything happened."

DAY SEVENTEEN

MONDAY, JUNE 22ND

Five miles southeast of Clinton, Maj. Charles Guess stood before a throng of reporters in the back of the old Cadyville Elementary School. He told them how investigators had developed more than 2,000 leads, and how law enforcement had looked into possible sightings in Steuben and Allegany counties, including a report of two men walking along the railroad bed in the town of Friendship. Officers had conducted a thorough canvas of the area with no success, and the search had since been redirected to the vicinity of a small hunting lodge in Owls Head.

What Guess did not say was that the events at Twisted Horn had brought on unforeseen pandemonium.

In the hours after Stockwell had reported the sighting, the New York State Police set up another command post closer to the cabin. With few options, they settled on the white four-door garage on Ragged Lake Road, home of the Owls Head-Mountain View Fire Department—but the small building had been unequipped to handle the chaos. More than one hundred troopers had flooded the stationhouse, wondering where to go next. Lack of cell and radio service had again hindered coordination with those bosses and underlings still out on the grounds of Twisted Horn. The higher-ups needed as many men and women as possible, but the sudden influx of personnel (and no place to put them) presented another logistical nightmare.

Guess already knew that this chaos was worth it. The DNA recovered from Stockwell's place was an exact match to that of the fugitives. But he was not prepared to let the public know—not just yet.

"We have developed evidence that the suspects may have spent time in a cabin in this area," he said into the bundle of microphones. "We have law enforcement officers from around the state and around the nation here today searching for more evidence. We cannot get into the specifics of the evidence we recovered while investigating this particular lead. We don't want to put information out in the public that could jeopardize our investigation."

A journalist piped up from the back of the crowd.

"It's already been reported widely that there is some sort of DNA—possibly evidence taken from that cabin out there from Owls Head," the reporter said. "So since it's already out there, the public is already aware of this, wouldn't it be beneficial at this point to at least confirm or deny whether or not you did in fact find some DNA evidence there?"

"We have recovered specific items from that cabin, we have forwarded them to the appropriate laboratories and reached conclusive determination," said Guess. "But we are not prepared to release that evidence at this time so we do not jeopardize the continuity of the investigation."

• • •

A man stood near the corner of Duane Road and County Route 27, signaling the two sergeants who had just driven past.

Cook spotted him and pulled over the car.

"What's going on over here?" he said.

"Sir, I haven't seen my neighbor in a couple of days but looks like his basement window might've been kicked in," the man said.

Cook gave a nod to his partner Rich White, who listened in from the passenger seat.

"Ok, we'll check it out."

The sergeants took out their firearms as they entered the house. The place had been left in disarray. Papers, clothes, and other odds and ends cluttered the ground level. It did not appear to have been lived in for some time.

The men searched though the darkened, dingy rooms before moving to the basement, then up to the second floor where they found two doors.

"I'll take this one, you take that one," Cook said. White nodded.

His gun still drawn, Cook went for the knob on the right. The hinge creaked as the door swung open.

The room appeared empty. He shined a light under the bed. Nothing.

Through the dimly lit space the sergeant noticed another door. "Probably be good to check the closet," he thought.

He reached out, turned the handle, and flung the door open.

On the other side stood a tall man, his hand on his gun, staring right back at him.

Cook reared back as if to raise his weapon when he realized the man was his partner.

"Holy Fuck, Rich! You scared the shit out of me!"

"I thought it was a closet!" said White. What they thought was a closet turned out to be a door connecting the two bedrooms. "Knew I heard something!"

Cook let out a long sigh of relief as they made their way back to the car to resume patrol. Each time he searched a house, cabin, barn, or shed, a series of physical responses were set in motion: a rapid heartbeat, a rush of adrenaline, a release of air once the place had been cleared. The sergeant entered every location as if the inmates were there—because they could be.

Maintaining a constant state of vigilance during long shifts and on little sleep had begun to take its toll on Cook and the other officers out in the field. The confirmed sighting at Twisted Horn had briefly boosted their morale, yet more than forty-eight hours had passed with no sign of the prisoners.

Cook heard his radio begin to sputter. Another call was coming in.

• • •

Sweat brought them to a halt. He pulled his coat over his head and shined a flashlight on his ball compass. They had put a few miles in between themselves and the cops, though the thick canopy made it impossible to navigate with the stars.

"Damnit," he thought, looking at the arrow. They had been heading too far east.

"Where's the road?" said Matt. He had lost sight of it in the dark.

"Up ahead."

They crossed, then redirected their course west before veering north, peppering the earth as they went. Miles later they reached a lodge in the middle of a clearing. Sweat searched rooms upstairs but found nothing useful. He went back down to where Matt was in the kitchen and began to open the cabinets.

"I already looked. There's no food."

"Did you check the fridge?"

"Yeah, no food."

Sweat had pulled the door back to see six MREs stacked inside. He guessed Matt had not checked that spot.

"I thought you said there was no food!"

Matt shrugged, betraying no signs of embarrassment.

They headed north again, and up over the mountain. (Sweat hoped this might throw off the troopers, who now knew they had been traveling west.) By high noon, the men stopped to rest by an old beaver pond.

Sweat handed Matt two of the MREs he had taken from the house.

"You should carry your own food in case something happens and we split up."

• • •

Michael McCaffrey (whose medieval wedding in the woods took place despite the growing manhunt) had called the state police twice to join the search. He had spent his childhood covered in camo in the woods of West Bangor, where he caught crayfish, tracked ky-oats, and threw knives at log targets. His fascination with survivalism continued into his mid-twenties, when he spent nine months camping out in the Adirondacks, surviving on frogs and boiled water. "The troopers from downstate are out of their element," McCaffrey thought. He knew the area and wanted to help in any way he could.

When the State Police declined his offers, McCaffrey took to social media.

"We know these woods better than law enforcement does," he wrote to his neighbors on Facebook. "I'm sick of being scared to go outside, of being ambushed for my car by fugitives desperate to remain free. I can't sit back and do nothing. Let's go get these guys!"

• • •

Matt and Sweat kept to the swamp's outer edge, where the footing was firm, until they reached a dam and overflowing brook. Sweat crossed first, using an uprooted tree as a bridge. From atop the knoll on the other side he could see an easier path for Matt. He directed him through the high vegetation to a boulder jutting out from the spring.

Sweat climbed down the bank and stood on another rock, his arms outstretched.

"Here, toss me your stuff, then jump."

Matt nodded, threw over his pack, then leaped. He just missed land, so Sweat pulled him up as he had done seventeen days before in Clinton's steam pipe.

They stopped to dry off, but their rest was quickly interrupted by the familiar thud of chopper blades.

Sweat looked up at the sky, then toward a mountain ahead.

"C'mon, let's go."

By dinnertime they had nearly reached the mountain's ridge. Matt found a place to sit while Sweat stood on top of a boulder, surveying the area. Within a minute he spotted a well-worn footpath.

"I'm going to go check it out," he said, placing his belongings next to Matt, who was quite happy to stay put.

Several trails ran along the side of this mountain, which Sweat later learned was named Elephant's Head. He chose the northern path and walked along until the trees parted in a breathtaking display: a valley where layers of leafy, dense wood extended along the slope to the waters of Lake Titus.

He hiked back to Matt.

"Dude, you've got to come see this! Grab your stuff!"

Matt went with reluctance. When he got there, he did not seem as impressed with the view, but he agreed that it was a decent spot to sit and eat the remainder of their MREs.

"There's a trail going west," Sweat said as he chewed. They had swapped a few items with one another like kids at a school lunch table. "We can go that way and try to find a few cabins."

Matt shrugged and sighed, the smell of booze on his breath.

"We should steal a boat and head up the lake," said Matt.

Sweat could not tell if he was kidding, serious, or just plain drunk.

"Are you crazy!?" He pointed to a patrol boat on the lake. "They're watching the water!"

Sweat knew a sober Matt would never suggest such a thing. He had seen him take periodic swigs from his new-found flask, yet for the number of sips he had taken, the container should have been empty by now. Sweat suspected his friend had another bottle stowed away in his pack, but he did not ask.

With their appetites temporarily satisfied, they traveled north down the crag. After hours of hiking they still had not stumbled upon a single camp.

"Fuck it. This shit is too long and we're starting to go the wrong way," Sweat said. "I'm getting tired."

"Me too."

"All right, we'll go back and sleep on the top of the mountain, and cross the swamp in the morning."

Matt shook his head.

"I'm not walking back up the hill."

Sweat had grown tired of these negotiations, but, again, did not want to argue.

"Then we'll walk off the trail and sleep."

They selected a strip of raised earth beneath an umbrella of branches. High above, the thump of blades beat like hands on a war drum.

• • •

BINGHAMTON, NEW YORK—JULY 3, 2002

Dave pulled his gold Honda up along Chenago. Shawn opened the back door and squeezed in, his long, slim legs pressing up against the passenger chair and into the small of Jeffrey Nabinger's back. Shawn knew Jeff from their childhood days on Liberty Street, and it was Jeff who had really introduced him to Dave. Law-breaking cohorts in and out of group homes since adolescence, Jeff and Dave were blood brothers in every sense of the phrase. They had recently procured several pricey weapons from Marino's Outdoor World, a gun shop forty-five miles east in the village of Hancock. The seamless burglary befuddled law enforcement; a witness reported seeing two men of slight builds sprint out of the store's shattered window, but police had yet to identify the suspects. Dave and Jeff had earned a sweet profit from the sale of their spoils, keeping only two semiautomatics from the acquired arsenal: a 9 mm Kahr for Jeff and a 40-caliber Glock for Dave. The success of the "Hancock thing," as Shawn later called it, bolstered their confidence, so much so that a similar plan was already in the works. Shawn had recently heard Jeff and Dave discuss breaking into Mess's Fireworks, a gun shop in Great Bend, Pennsylvania. They had scouted out the place several times to acquaint themselves with the terrain and determine which door led to the pistols, assault rifles, and other potential loot. Shawn was more in favor of Jeff's original proposal to rob the Taco Bell where he used to work, but Dave said no. Weapons were worth more.

The warm July wind swept through the sunroof as Dave handled the curves with smooth expertise. He had spent significant time tinkering with the engine and fine-tuning the accelerator of his 1990 Accord, and Shawn felt the difference. Dave knew his way around machines, which proved useful; he was a seasoned carjacker before he could lawfully drive. But for the last two months he and Jeff had laid low, killing time at their place—15 Dickinson Street, the last house on a dead-end block. On any given night, the three Binghamton boys would most likely be found sitting on the floor or the desk chair or the weight bench in the Dickinson den, passing joints and the controller of Dave's PlayStation 2, each taking turns stealing vehicles and gunning down cops in Grand Theft Auto III. Or they might be found in a secluded, forested spot Dave named One Dirt Road, part of a concealed path behind Felchar Manufacturing Co. in the neighboring town of Kirkwood. That was their present destination.

Dave wheeled the Honda toward the yard of stolen property: two Ford Broncos, an F-150 Monster Truck, a boxy Ford Econoline Van, and a 1979 Winnebago, the latest addition to the trove of steel loot strategically placed far from the thoroughfare. They took a few hits as they looked over a hand-drawn map of Mess. At 11:15 p.m., their firearms holstered at the hip—the Khar for Jeff, the Glock for Dave, and a 9 mm Smith & Wesson from Marino's for Shawn—they resumed their former positions in the Accord and sped off.

DAY EIGHTEEN

TUESDAY, JUNE 23RD

The rustic Upper Lodge of Titus Mountain Family Ski Center had transformed into what looked like a 24-7 military base. Large maps of the Adirondacks hung above long folding tables strewn with laptops, radios, and lukewarm coffee. Each law enforcement agency had a designated space in the room, where field teams congregated to strategize.

In his twenty-six years of working on the slopes, general manager Zachary White had never seen anything like it. He had been approached by the Troop B Emergency Management NCO Chad Niles after the State Police confirmed a DNA match at Twisted Horn. His men and women needed more space than the Owls Head-Mountain View Fire Department could provide, and this venue had the capacity to be headquarters for the manhunt. With White's blessing, the troops began to move in. Hundreds of generators and portable light towers had been brought onto the resort's lot. Trailers, Humvees, trucks, and four wheelers had parked on the lawn where Bell UH-1H choppers would also land to refuel. Two radio antennas had been set up on Titus—a range made up of three interconnected mountains, the upper, middle, and lower peaks—to improve communication. At its busiest, more than three hundred personnel packed underneath the rafters to eat, wash up, and receive their next orders.

The fifty-two-year-old manager, a tall man with broad shoulders and a deep voice accustomed to delegating, assembled a crew to help feed the small army. Each day White was at work by 5 a.m., brewing some forty gallons of coffee to prepare for the morning briefing. The 6 a.m. rundown of the day's game plan—with updates on recovered evidence and other intel, as well as a medical rundown warning against deer ticks and diseases like giardiasis—was presented every morning.[37] Downstate troopers staying in the dormitories of Paul Smith's College and SUNY Plattsburgh were bussed in to attend the meeting, where a projector had been set up so that the crowd could view a map of what areas had been cleared and which spots needed their attention.

As White prepared the day's meals (mostly hamburgers, goulash, pulled pork sandwiches, Glaziers hot dogs, and peanut butter and jelly, items donated by locals and area businesses), and the pack was about to break for duty, a boss called out to the crowd: "Be careful, keep your eyes open, don't get hurt. You've got the right to shoot. Don't take any chances."

---

37 Giardiasis is an infection in the small intestine, caused by a parasite. It is typically contracted through drinking untreated water.

• • •

Five miles southwest of the headquarters, Sweat placed his hand in the cove at the base of Titus Mountain. He let the cool waves lap over his palm. He thought back to each time he had gone fishing with his Uncle Jimmy. He never thought he would see a body of fresh water like this again.

Matt caught up and they headed east around the lake until dense marshland forced them to halt. (They had stopped only once before, at a secluded picnic area with a shed where they had taken a hot chocolate packet, two black garbage bags, and a handful of pepper.) Seeing no way around, Sweat peeled off his rain jacket and slid it in his pack.

"I think I'm just going to put my stuff in a garbage bag and swim across," he said.

"Go ahead in," said Matt, who did not seem enthused.

Sweat felt his pockets for the bags.

"Did I give them to you?"

"No," Matt said.

"Shit, I must've dropped them. Fuck it, I guess we're going through the swamp [like this] then."

Limbs outstretched like two high-wire artists, they waded through the sludge, their feet feeling for solid ground. Slipping all the way in could mean being swallowed by a sinkhole.

Once across, they hiked north toward an uneven utility road lined with cabins in the distance. Sweat waited for Matt, who had again fallen behind. Sweat guessed he had a good buzz going.

Just as Matt caught up, Sweat spotted a white vehicle parked up a few yards away.

"Get down!" he yelled. "Looks like a sheriff's truck!"

Through the trees Sweat could make out a man in camo gear. He guessed the officer—if it *was* an officer—would try to outflank them. Either way, he did not want to find out.

Sweat pointed to the way they had come.

"Go!" he hissed, rising to stand.

Matt ran a few steps but stopped. Sweat was a few paces ahead when he noticed his partner had fallen several paces behind. He turned back, urging him to come.

"C'mon!"

Matt stumbled along in a circle. Sweat gave him a hard look.

"He's walking like he does not care," he thought.

Sweat began to sprint again before glancing back. From afar he could make out a green and black dot drifting slowly into oblivion.

"Fuck this," Sweat said aloud, and took off.

• • •

To his frustration, Cook had been assigned to a fixed post near the corner of County Route 27 and Duane Road in Chasm Falls. He had just found a rhythm with his roving team when they were abruptly pulled apart and delegated to static positions in the detail. Cook understood the need for these posts; the State Police had to maintain a fixed presence along the established perimeter, and stop cars and search trunks for any sign of the inmates. But he knew his men could be more efficient driving from place to place vetting complaints than those troopers brought in from out of town. The downstate guys did not know the lay of the land. Communication had improved only slightly with the addition of portable radio towers. Through no fault of their own, these troopers might spend more time searching for a GPS signal than responding to a call. He knew selecting certain personnel for specific jobs would not be a priority when the bosses had Albany breathing down their necks. They had one primary goal: saturate the area with as many of their people as possible and hope they could find the two needles in the haystack.

• • •

Sweat stopped his sprint at the edge of a two-lane blacktop road. He had run for what felt like miles. Catching his wind, he crept up behind the brush to see a state prison box truck drive by. He glanced down to the left, then the right before sprinting across into a cluster of felled trees. He went to climb the mound for a better view but slipped on the bark and skidded down the pile. Pushing himself up, he gave it another go only to slide again, this time landing square on his back.

Sweat slipped a third time before finding his footing in the mess of tangled tree limbs. Once on solid ground, he headed north at a fast jog, whizzing past a swamp to the west and a hill to the east. Blood pounded through his body, nourishing his limbs with endless endurance; he felt so light that he barely noticed the weight of his pack as he fled through the forest. As he ran, he heard a four wheeler up over a hill, then a car and doors and a barking dog. Without stopping, he took the bag of pepper out of his right pocket and rubbed the seasoning into his skin. (He had no idea if this was throwing the search dogs off his scent; he hoped it was doing *something*.) He then began to follow the river, slowing his pace only to dip his hat in the water to cool off before speeding up once more.

He kept on like this until he saw troopers parked on a bridge that passed over a narrow brook. He hunkered down, kneeling among the rocks to listen. As soon as the vehicles pulled away, he dashed across the water, hopping from boulder to boulder back into the shelter of the woods.

As the sun fell, Sweat slowed his pace, walking several more miles before reaching a high embankment. He peered over the mound, which was on the outer edge of a farmer's field. If anyone was in the house situated on this property, they would not be able to see him from this distance. And so he stayed, dozing off until night fell.

Upon waking, Sweat took to the road again. He trudged along the blacktop, slowed somewhat by the gaping sores in his heels, raw from the day's running. Hours passed before he came across another house built near a sprawling field of corn. He supposed its tenants were still asleep; the moon was only just beginning to wane. He decided to camp out among the husks until after dawn.

As the burgeoning leaves swayed with a gentle breeze, his own thoughts drifted back to Matt. He wondered where he was, what he was doing, and, most of all, what would become of him now.

• • •

HALLSTEAD, PENNSYLVANIA—JULY 3, 2002

Dave had driven around Hallstead for more than an hour before spotting a vehicle suitable for the job. He pulled his gold Accord up to the green F-150, a recent trade-in at Fuccillo Ford, and got out to have a look. Satisfied with the find, he and Jeff took out a screwdriver and began to loosen the truck's steering column. Shawn could hear the pounding from the back seat of the Honda, where he had remained until the two had successfully broken the ignition.

"That's it," Jeff said before climbing into the driver's seat of the stolen truck. "Let's go."

Shawn began to feel apprehensive about the whole thing.

"It's not a good idea to do this. I've got a bad feeling there's something bad gonna happen. Something's going to go wrong."

Dave shook his head. "You're paranoid."

Shawn looked out the window. He was perturbed that his friend did not take him seriously. Yet in a way, he understood where Dave was coming from. The plan was well-thought out; Dave and Jeff had staked out Marino's several times. They had done their homework, Shawn told himself, as convincingly as he could. It would go just like Hancock—without a hitch.

DAY NINETEEN

WEDNESDAY, JUNE 24TH

A rustle came from within the cornfield. Sweat, who had still been asleep, opened his eyes to see a doe pushing her nose through the crop. He felt the thump of her hooves through the ground as she inched gently towards him, but he quickly shooed her away. Seemingly stung by his rebuff, she bleated back before retreating into the maize.

Sweat looked toward the sky to see that the sun was already high. "I must have slept too late," he thought. He had missed his opportunity to scout out the house on the edge of the field. There was no going over there now.

Sweat packed his bag and headed north through the woods until he came across a large road. From behind the dense brush, he scanned the blacktop. Several cars from highway patrol drove by while he waited, although they did not seem to notice his presence. Once the coast was clear he began to walk again, keeping in line with the road until he crossed back into the woods. From there he followed a truck trail, which led down to another part of the road, over a creek, and up a hill. He stopped only once for a quick bite before reaching a short bridge that spanned over a small swamp.

Day had turned to dusk by the time Sweat spotted a cabin. He had seen several police cars drive by throughout the last eight hours or so, as he was not far from the main road, so he lingered in the thick before approaching the dwelling.

He tried the front entrance (locked) and the back door (also locked), and so began to survey the windows of the enclosed porch. He chose one where the screen had been nailed into the rotting wood of its sill, and pried it open with relative ease.

The place looked much like any of the others, furnished with a modest table and chairs, with a small kitchen to the right. Sweat unplugged the refrigerators (there were two) before opening the door, as lights on the appliances might be visible from the road. He took a few items—two Pepsi Max sodas, a pack of frozen hot dogs, two ham, cheese, and egg Hot Pockets, some Butterfinger eggs, and a few pickled eggs—along with the fanny pack, thermal foil blanket, and pair of emergency hand warmers he found in the main room. Sweat had also considered taking thirty-five dollars he discovered in the fridge (why they kept the money there was beyond him) but ultimately decided against it.

As he began to devour the pickled eggs, a blinding light passed through the windows. He kneeled below the height of the panes as the beam grew brighter.

• • •

GREAT BEND, PENNSYLVANIA—JULY 4, 2002

Jeff steered the stolen truck toward Mess's Fireworks with Dave and Shawn in the bed. They had left the Honda less than ten miles away in Grange Hall Park in Kirkwood, New York, which they would retrieve once they had their loot.

It was in the middle of the night in Independence Day when the boys finally arrived at the gun shop. Jeff drove by a few times to scout the place out; the last thing they wanted was to run into anyone.

Seeing no one, Jeff pulled into the lot and swung the truck around so that the tailgate faced the large storefront window. He threw the truck in reverse and hit the gas. Shawn and Dave gripped the sides of the bed as the vehicle slammed into the windows.

The impact cracked the pane, but it remained mostly intact. Jeff put the truck in drive, pulled ahead, and threw it in reverse again.

Shawn and Dave slid across the bed as shards of glass flew through the air.

"Holy shit!" Shawn screamed.

They jumped out of the truck. Shawn went to the left towards the pistol case and began grabbing the weapons. The weight of the metal gave him a strange feeling. He had never fired a gun before, and if he got the chance, the most he would want to do is shoot a tin can.

DAY TWENTY

THURSDAY, JUNE 25TH

At 6 a.m., Franz Fredericks strode the length of the long driveway that was attached to the three-story log house he had built on Titus Mountain. Over the past few days, the slender, seventy-three-year-old hardware salesman had noticed a number of troopers posted every fifty feet along Fayette Road—the southeast border of his eighty-eight-acre plot that extended east toward Chasm Falls. News had spread that the inmates might be somewhere in the area, but he had not been too bothered. "They don't want to encounter me," he thought, "and I don't want to encounter them."

Fredericks had been on his way to Plattsburgh when he first heard of the prison break. He was traveling east along Route 374 and planned to drive through Dannemora that day when state troopers had stopped him and turned him around. The businessman had attempted to reach the city through the backroads, but those too were blocked off. Fredericks had never seen anything like it. He had never heard of an escape from Clinton—at least not in his lifetime.

At the end of the drive he picked up his copy of the Malone Telegram, took the paper back to his front door, and handed it off to his partner Betsy before going outside once more. Nearly every morning he would join his dog Henry for their daily one-hour hike up Mt. Titus. It was a stroll Fredericks looked forward to and never feared; there was not one square inch of his property he did not know by heart.

Yet on this morning, as he moved toward the edge of the woods, an unfamiliar feeling passed through him. As the salesman looked toward the trees with uncharacteristic trepidation, Henry began to bark. It was a sound Fredericks rarely heard out of the gentle beast, who now paced from side to side, pausing between snarls to listen, his fur standing on end.

It might have been nothing, but Fredericks suspected that someone who had no business being there was somewhere just past where he could see.

"Well," he said to himself. "I don't think I'll walk the mountain today."

• • •

Sweat remained huddled in his hiding place as headlights flooded the dark cabin. He could hear the door of a vehicle swing shut, and the sound of voices that seemed to belong to the troopers.

One of them began to approach. Sweat stayed crouched, barely breathing.

The cop shined a flashlight into the windows. The beam roved over the furniture, the walls, and the wooden planks before it turned back outside. Sweat could hear the shuffle of boots, then the slam of a car door. The headlights began to fade.

He waited a few minutes, then went out the way he came.

Through the night Sweat continued to follow the road until—to his surprise—he walked straight onto the grass of the Malone Golf Club. He took the opportunity to refill his water bottles there, though he did not linger, heading back into the forest for a quick nap and a small meal of one soda and a Butterfinger egg. He continued on, climbing a steep hill overgrown with elder pines, tramping over the fallen needles as he made his way southwest toward the steep embankment. The hike had left him soaked with perspiration, so he removed his soiled tank top and wet socks, drying them out before carrying on once more.

There had been more close encounters with civilians and law enforcement that morning than any other in the last twenty days. A golf cart on the course, a white SUV on the hill, a four wheeler in the woods, and more state troopers driving by on Duane Road—all suggested that he had come too close to town. Each had jolted him enough that he began to jog north, moving as fast as his legs would carry him. He only stopped at one cabin to replenish his supply (there he nicked a pair of binoculars, honey-roasted peanuts, and a few dollar bills) before restarting his journey. He sprinted by a cluster of trees, through a field, past a small pen of beef cattle grazing by a white farmhouse, and over a large dip in the land, veering northeast to cross Duane. Through more fields and over more roads he ran like there was no tomorrow.

Sweat kept on at this steady clip until he approached what looked like a traffic light in the distance. He watched, listening for movement up ahead. He had come to downtown Malone by the looks of it; a number of homes with modest plots sat close together along the edge of the road. Seeing no cars, he darted across and turned right toward a white house with a "For Sale" sign posted on the property. As soon as the street was clear—and taking care to avoid a neighbor next door who had stepped out to move his black Toyota truck—he shot across the front yard and into the back of the house for sale, down another embankment that led to the strong current of the Salmon River.

Sweat followed the water until it opened into a small field bordered by a white fence. He stopped there to wash himself and paused for a moment's rest. Through his new binoculars he could see the neat row of homes and manicured lawns.

Freedom from prison life did not mean he was a free man. He did not belong to the prison world anymore, but he did not belong to this one either. Here he was considered a wanted man—a murderer, a monster, an outlaw.

Sweat heard the sound of sirens. He turned the binoculars toward the noise and saw two cop cars driving past.

"Shit," he thought. "I hope those aren't for Matt."

• • •

Sandy Oneill stood outside her home on Reservoir Road in Cadyville, less than five miles from Dannemora. The sixty-six-year-old had talked with her neighbor Gene Palmer just a few days before. They had discussed law enforcement, the prison, and the government as a whole, to which the CO closed the conversation with one final thought: "If they want ya, they're going to get ya."

These words returned to her now, hours after Palmer's arrest.

"He did not know," she told a journalist who had knocked on her door. "I would swear on my father's grave he did not know these guys were going to escape."

Word had spread over the weekend that the state police were looking into the conduct of a corrections officer and his role in the Clinton escape. With an investigation under-way, the CO had been placed on administrative leave. Two state troopers had been posted at the end of Palmer's drive to keep tabs on him before he was brought into police cus-tody. During questioning, he admitted that he had received paintings from Matt, had allowed the inmates to venture out on the catwalks behind their cells, had provided them with needle nose pliers, and had approved a box of raw hamburger meat (which, unbeknownst to Palmer, con-tained drill bits and hacksaw blades from Joyce) to enter the facility without first passing through a metal detector.

The state police had charged him with two counts of tampering with physical evidence—both felonies—and one count of official misconduct, a misdemeanor. (Another count of promoting prison contraband would be tacked on later.) He had appeared in Plattsburgh Town Court the night before and was held on $25,000 bail. He had pleaded not guilty on all charges, and his formal arraignment was slated for Thursday, June 25.

But by Thursday afternoon, Andrew Brockway, a small-town attorney who had stepped up to represent the guard, had asked the judge to postpone the date.

"I'm a solo practitioner. This is taking a lot of resources. I really believe in Mr. Palmer and I think he needs a team of attorneys that have the resources that he's going to need to fight these charges," he told a throng of reporters outside the courthouse, holding up his hand to show them a wristband that the CO had given him. Inscribed on the blue rubber bracelet were the words, "Clinton Strong."

Brockway said Palmer had been truthful during questioning and had even passed a polygraph test.

"Mr. Palmer has continued to cooperate. I admire him, I consider him a friend, and I wish him nothing but the best."

Oneill too considered him a friend. Palmer had lived next door to her for ten years, along with his longtime girlfriend, Mary Lamar, also a corrections officer at Clinton. After the escape, Palmer had even taken the time to caution his neighbors about venturing out alone. "I just want to give you a heads up—they believe they're in this area," he had told them. "Don't go walking in the woods by yourself."

"There's a lot of people he feels he's let down," Oneill said. "I told him he has not. Everybody is with him 100 percent."

She looked up at the reporter, then paused for a moment before speaking again.

"There's a lot more that are going to go down than just Gene."

• • •

Fredericks felt the foundation of his three-story log house begin to shake. He opened his eyes to see that his dark bedroom was now as bright as day.

A low, repetitious thud drew his gaze upward. Through the skylight above the bed where he still lay, a helicopter hovered so low that he thought it might land on the roof. Its spotlight passed over the house, then through the room's double glass door. He rolled out of bed and stood near the window to see the chopper's beam was now scanning the forest floor.

For more than an hour it circled the sky as Fredericks watched, wondering what they had seen out in the woods.

KIRKWOOD, NEW YORK—JULY 4, 2002

The entire job at Mess's took less than three minutes. By 3:30 a.m. the Binghamton boys had returned to Grange Hall Park and began to transfer the weapons from the bed of the truck to the Honda.

Shawn pulled out a cigarette and smoked half before passing the rest to Jeff, who passed it to Dave. They had gotten away with it; they hadn't seen anyone. They made off like bats out of hell. But the ordeal had shaken Shawn, and he hoped the nicotine would have a calming effect.

As they loaded up the car, a pair of headlights came down the road. Even from the darkened lot, Shawn recognized their shape.

"Cop!" one of the others yelled.[38]

Jeff and Shawn ran back toward the bushes. Dave climbed underneath the front of the truck as the officer pulled in.

---

38 Sweat maintains that he did not yell out "cop." He also does not recall Jeff Nabinger calling out the word.

DAY TWENTY-ONE

FRIDAY, JUNE 26TH

U.S. Border Patrol agent Chris Voss received a call that shots had been fired off Route 30 near Lake Titus. He and other members of his tactical unit headed toward the scene as reports of more shots came over the line. When Voss arrived, a state trooper on patrol said they had heard coughing coming from deep in the woods.

The border patrol team began to close in when Voss saw movement through the trees.

"Show your hands!" he yelled.

He heard the branches rustle. Voss inched toward the sound.

A man's face became visible through the brush. As Voss approached, he could see the barrel of a twenty-gauge shotgun pointed directly at him.

He drew his M4 and fired.

• • •

Sgt. Jay Cook drove along Frenette Road six miles east of Lake Titus.

"Boy," he thought, looking out the window to a passing farm field. "Imagine if they just came running out of there."

Not a moment later his phone rang.

Cook answered. The voice of one of his men came across the line.

"Hey, d'ya hear what's going on!?" the trooper said. "They just shot one of 'em!"

"You're fucking kidding me!" Cook said. He had not heard a word of it on the radio. "Damn reception!" he thought.

"The major wants you down on Route 30, Trombley Road. Set up a road block."

"O.K.," Cook said.

The sergeant switched on his AVL—the automatic vehicle location technology used by the New York State Police to view the positions of other personnel in the area. A sea of blue dots spread across the screen. The specks represented the hundreds of troopers who had surrounded Route 30 near Lake Titus in Elephant's Head, several miles east of Chasm Falls off Fayette Road.

Cook took in the digital display. He had never seen so many officers in one place. Later one of his colleagues would print out the image and hang it up in the barracks, an homage to those who partook in the manhunt that would forever change the tiny town of Malone.

• • •

Franz Fredericks was heading home from his hardware shop when he reached a checkpoint at the dam of Chasm Falls near the corner of Studley Hill Road, five miles east of Route 30 on Mt. Titus.

An officer approached his vehicle.

"You can't go home," said the cop.

Fredericks checked the time. Betsy would be expecting him for supper.

"Well, how long's this going to take?" he asked.

The cop shook his head.

"We don't know."

Fredericks waited on the side of the road. The salesman, whose demeanor was more gentle and good-natured than most, did not complain. Instead he thought back to his dog Henry, who had barked at something in the woods just one day before.

• • •

Greg Durandetto was on shift at the assembly line at the General Motors plant in Tonawanda, New York, when another worker caught his attention.

"Hey," the latter said. "I'm sorry to hear about your friend."

Durandetto paused.

"What are you talking about, Stu?"

"Richard Matt. You know him, right? Didn't you hear? They shot him in the head."

Durandetto had not heard. He did he know what to think.

"There was no way he was going back to prison," he later said. "Death by cop was better than going back."

• • •

Michael McCaffrey rode in the passenger seat as his wife Terry drove their purple Subaru Tribeca along Route 30. As soon as he heard about the shooting, he had pulled on his 3D leafy camo ghillie suit and stuffed his metal framed military-style ALICE pack with a tarp, headlamp, maps, three trail cams, a canteen, battery packs, a bush knife, and other camping tools. He had not had luck rallying a crew of locals to join in the search, and the state police did not seem to want his assistance, but no matter. McCaffrey was prepared to go at it alone.

"I hope they don't shoot Sweat," he said to his wife before leaving the car. "I want to hear that goddamn story."

• • •

Cheers erupted in the upper lodge of Titus Mountain Family Ski Center. Troopers and other members of law enforcement hugged and shook hands. Word had spread that Richard Matt was dead.

Not five minutes later, manager Zach White's phone buzzed in his pocket. His sister had sent him a text message from her home near Heidelberg, Germany. Even thousands of miles away, she too had heard the news.

• • •

Sweat lay still on the floor of a deer blind, lost in thought.

He had spent most of the day hiking north through dense marshland before coming across this bit of shelter, where he decided to spend the night. As he prepared to sleep he turned on his transistor radio and hung the device from a nail on the wall. He was about to drift off when heard a voice come over the waves:

Richard Matt has been killed.

Sweat was brought back to full alertness. He listened intently.

Shots had been heard near Lake Titus, the voice said. Law enforcement had found a bullet hole in a trailer. Troopers had saturated the area. A border patrol agent had shot Matt in the head. A special team had been flown in to remove his body.

Sweat could now hear the faint, familiar whir of chopper blades.

"You dumbass," he thought. "What the hell did you fire at an RV for?"

Part of Sweat did not believe the story about how things went down, but it really didn't matter. Matt was dead.

The words from just a few days before came swimming back into focus:

"You've got to make it if I don't," his friend had said.

"Dude, stop saying you're not going to make it."

"Just promise me."

"C'mon, motherfucker, I'm ready to go."

"If you want to go, go, but I'm not leaving 'til dark. I'm not going to get caught or killed because you want to drink. I'll go my own fucking way first."

"Well if you feel that way then you should just shoot me in the head."

BINGHAMTON, NEW YORK—JULY 4, 2002
3:45 A.M.

The police car pulled into the parking lot of Grange Hall Park. Sheriff Deputy Kevin Tarsia stepped out of the vehicle. He worked the night shifts and would often stop home for dinner, a quarter of a mile down the road. But something in the park drew him in. Perhaps it was the Honda and the stolen truck (or the presence of the young men, if he could see them in the night) that made him veer off course. Perhaps it was simply a sense of duty.

Tarsia shined a spotlight toward the vehicles. He stepped out of his patrol car, a flashlight in one hand and a 40-caliber Glock in the other.

Dave drew his gun.

Then the shots came, ringing through the dark:

Bang. Bang. Bang. Bang. Bang. Bang. Bang. Bang. Bang. Bang. Bang. Bang. Bang. Bang. Bang.

He had emptied his clip.

Shawn and Jeff peered out from behind the bushes. Dave was on his feet. He was still holding the Glock. In that moment—in that single second when the world had slowed down, when it seemed to have closed in and swallowed him whole—Shawn realized it was Dave who had shot the sheriff's deputy.

Dave jumped in the Honda and hit the gas. The cop, who

had been knocked to the ground, went to reach for his own Glock before the wheels rolled over his body, dragging him across the asphalt.

The car stopped. Jeff watched from behind the nearby brush.

Shawn's head pounded. He could not comprehend what had just happened—and he did not want to. He did not want to be there. He wished he had never come.

DAY TWENTY-TWO

Sweat woke up at dawn. It took a few seconds before he remembered Matt was dead.

He lay in the deer blind contemplating what more he could have done, but just as quickly put his feelings aside. He would deal with those later. The hunt was still on and he needed to move.

Sweat headed north down a hill and around a swamp, following a path into a field that appeared to have been recently logged. More woods led him past a small brook to the edge of a farm, where he found a trail that led him to a makeshift wooden ship—a prop assembled in Memorial Recreation Park by members of a local theater group, the Ekrub Players.[39]

Another trail brought him to another farm field, where he found something that struck him as rather odd: a hole

---

39 Ekrub is "Burke" spelled backwards. The theater group is based in Burke, New York.

in the ground about seven feet deep and twelve feet across, where a large TV box, an old vacuum cleaner, and several plastic bags of clothing had been placed. Sweat jumped in to have a look around. He came across a brown shirt with the words "Church of Burke: Doing Whatever It Takes to Connect People to God."

He took the shirt and had just climbed out when he heard the sound of an ATV from down the trail. Seeing no other place to hide, he slid back into the hole, curled up, and sat under the TV box until the four wheeler passed.

For the next seven miles Sweat headed northeast. He stopped once for lunch (a quarter stick of pepperoni he retrieved from his pack) and again at the edge of the Little Trout River. He paused only a moment before he heard voices carry through the wood.

Pulling his hood over his head, Sweat peered from behind a tree. The river cascaded down to a pool where several people were playing in the falls. From his hiding spot, he watched them leave as more people arrived. One pretty woman whose pink swimsuit hugged her curves posed for a photo. She was so close to where he sat that he wondered if he had been captured in the frame.

Hours passed before he set off again, continuing north toward the town of Burke. Once far enough away from the falls, he got out his map and decided to follow Finney Road west toward Route 11—the same highway he and Matt had planned to take to Mexico.

• • •

BINGHAMTON, NEW YORK—JULY 3, 2002
3:46 A.M.

Jeff stood over the body of the sheriff's deputy, who continued to flail. One of Dave's bullets had pierced the man's belly. It seemed the others had missed, their shell casings scattered across the asphalt.

Jeff pointed his 9 mm Khar at the cop.

BANG.

An unexpected thud made Jeff look down. The weapon's magazine had released, falling to the ground.

Jeff bent down and picked up the cop's Glock. He aimed its barrel at the face of the sheriff's deputy and shot again at point blank range.

BANG. BANG.

Shawn froze.

Jeff walked coolly over to the patrol car and took the keys out of the ignition. He then popped the trunk and began to rifle through the deputy's belongings. He swiped the arrest forms and traffic flares and stashed them in the stolen truck.

Shawn ran out toward the Honda, opened the back door, and jumped in. He sat glued to the seat of the car, unable to process what he had just seen as he looked out the passenger window at Kevin Tarsia's limp body.

"I want to get out of here," he thought. "I don't want to be here, I don't want anybody to know we're here, let's get out of here, let's go before anybody finds us, maybe we gotta chance to still get out of this."

DAY TWENTY-THREE

At lunch time, Cook returned to the Malone barracks with a six-inch Subway chicken sandwich. (The woman ahead of him in line had seen him in uniform and purchased his meal. "We appreciate what you guys are doing and we just wish you the best of luck," she had told him before wrapping her arms around his neck in a warm embrace.) He had spent the morning vetting complaints, and now was prepared to patrol beyond the main search area just north of town.

White had the day off, so Cook invited his station commander and longtime friend, Sgt. Audra Parent, to come along.

"Hey, you want to come out and patrol for a while?" he asked.

At first, Parent, a petite, attractive woman with short blonde curls, said yes. But then she thought better of it.

"Eh no, I've got too much work to do," she said.

"C'mon! I don't have anybody with me today. You should come."

She smiled and shook her head.

"Nah, I have to do the casebook. I can't."

Cook groaned. He could not believe she wanted to do paperwork at a time like this. How could anyone stay back at the barracks in the middle of a manhunt?

"All right, fine!" he said with a smile. "I'll have to go fucking get him myself!"

• • •

Sweat woke from a nap near the corner of Route 11 and Finney Road. Earlier he had stopped off at an empty house, which he thought must be owned by a hair stylist, as a cozy two-chair salon had been built inside. The kitchen was well-stocked: he toasted two French bread pizzas, drank a few glugs of whole milk, downed several pickles, and packed away a number of other items—a block of sliced cheese, lunch meat, smoked sausages, hot chocolate, two bottles of water, breakfast bars, Pop Tarts, Chips Ahoy! cookies, Ritz crackers, several cans of tuna fish, and a mini pack of peanut M&Ms he found in the pantry. The place had been a lucky discovery. In another day he would be in Canada, and he did not know when he would come across this much food again.

He continued north towards Hawks Hollow until he reached Route 122. Through his binoculars he could see cars driving east and west along the highway.

Once he saw a break in the traffic, he sprinted across the two lanes and nearly tumbled down a steep embankment and into a shallow creek. Hopping from boulder to logs, he worked his way over the water and hiked to the edge of a field.

His plan was to spend the day surveying the border. It was only a few miles north, but it might be heavily guarded, Sweat thought. He needed to determine its weakest point before attempting to cross.

He passed through more farmland until he reached Coveytown Road. An open field lay beyond the blacktop.

Sweat looked farther north and saw a line of trees. "Those will provide good cover," he thought.

But just then, a state trooper zoomed past.

Sweat hung back. He watched and waited until the trooper drove off.

Now was his chance to make for the tree line. He began to walk through the alfalfa field—yet not halfway across, he again heard the sound of an engine.

He looked over his shoulder. A trooper had pulled his Crown Vic to the side of the road.

Sweat threw his head back to the skies.

"You've got to be fucking kidding me."

• • •

Cook drove his Crown Vic north along Shears Road in Constable, then to Poplar Street in the same direction until he reached Coveytown Road. For a few minutes he debated which way to go. "Probably best to make a loop around Burke," he thought, and opted to turn right and head east.

A light mist had settled on his windshield. The sergeant rolled down his window for a better view. He passed an abandoned railroad bed and a graduation party out on someone's front lawn, inching along as he scanned the fields.

Then, some five hundred yards away, he saw a backpack and a flash of camo.

"What the hell!?" Cook exclaimed aloud.

He sped up to get a closer look. Through a small opening in the brush he could make out a man moving north through the alfalfa field.

"*It can't be him,*" Cook thought. "*It's the middle of the day.*"

The sergeant called out his open window.

"Hey!" he yelled.

The man turned, pausing a moment before making a motion with his arms.

Cook shouted again.

"Get over here! Come here!"

But the man did not come. He kept swinging his arms, now hollering something that Cook could not hear.

"*Is he trying to bluff me?*" he wondered.

The sergeant threw the car in park.

"Get over here!" he yelled again.

As soon as Cook opened the car door, the man began to run.

• • •

Sweat froze. He heard the cop call out, but he could not make out the words.

"Nah, I'm good, bro!" he shouted.

"Come here!" the officer yelled.

227

Sweat threw up his arms and began to walk away.

The sound of a car door opening carried across the field. He glanced back to see the cop standing in the middle of the road.

Sweat bolted.

"Shit!" he heard the cop roar.

Sweat knew he could run for a long time, but his pack was heavy; it would slow him down. He slid it off without breaking his stride. He had everything he needed on him. He could get the rest again.

He sped up. The distance between him and the trooper had grown.

"*I have to make it to the woods,*" he told himself. "*I just have to make it to the woods.*"

The sound of quickened steps beat behind him.

"Stop or I'll shoot!" the cop cried out.

"*There's no way this guy can catch me. If I can just make it to the woods…*"

"Stop or I'll shoot!" he hollered.

Sweat put his arms out.

"Don't shoot me, I don't have a weapon!" he called back.

Sweat kept running.

A shot rang out.

• • •

"*It's fucking him.*"

The sergeant drew out his pistol. He dashed out of the car with the door wide open, his keys still in the ignition.

"B1-01, I need a unit!" Cook called over the radio as he ran. "Foot pursuit, Coveytown Road, Constable…"

He did not know if the transmission went through. He just kept running.

"STOP!" Cook bellowed.

The man glanced over, then rolled his shoulders back. His bag dropped to the ground.

Cook sprinted. He kept both hands on the gun.

"Stop or I'm going to shoot ya!"

The man sped up.

"*I'm not going to catch him*," thought the sergeant. "*He's headed for the woods.*"

"If you don't stop I'm going to shoot!"

The man called out something but Cook could not make out the words.

The sergeant stopped some forty-five yards short of his target. He raised his gun. He tilted his back, lined up his sights, and aimed at the dot of blurry camo.

He squeezed the trigger.

For a moment, the whole world went silent.

• • •

The first bullet struck Sweat's shoulder. He looked down. His right arm flopped against his body.

"*Shit*," he thought.

He raced for the trees.

The second shot rang. Hot metal pierced his back and blew straight through his lung.

Sweat fell to the ground.

"Put your hands out to your sides! Put your hands out to your sides!" the officer yelled.

"I can't! It doesn't work!" Sweat said, looking at his lifeless arm.

Blood began to fill his throat. He used his left hand to start pushing himself up off the ground.

"Don't fucking move or I'll shoot you again!"

Sweat looked over at the cop. He spat out a glob of blood.

"I have to sit up," he choked. "I can't breathe."

Everything went dark.

• • •

Cook did not hear the gun go off. He did not feel the kick. The only sound was a distant dull thump of a bullet striking a body.

From across the field he saw the man's right arm fall limp.

Again, Cook held his sights and squeezed the trigger.

THUD.

The man went down and the world came back into focus.

The sergeant sprinted over to David Sweat. An empty knife sheath hung from the fugitive's right hip. A ball compass was pinned to the inside of his left breast pocket, which had flapped open. Blood had soaked through his heavy camo coat.

Sweat began to push himself up.

"Don't you move or I'll shoot you again," the sergeant said before holding up the radio to his lips. Blood started to spurt out of Sweat's mouth.

"Suspect is down," Cook called over to dispatch. "I need a medical bag."

Near his feet, Sweat groaned.

"I just wanted to be free," Sweat said softly. "I just wanted to disappear."

Cook stood over him in silence. He could already hear the sirens.

BINGHAMTON, NEW YORK—JULY 3, 2002 3:50 A.M.

The tires screeched as Dave peeled out of the parking lot. Jeff sat in the front. Shawn was in the back seat. They left the truck behind.

"I'm sorry, I'm sorry," Dave said again and again.

His voice began to crack before he fell silent. It was too dark to know for sure, but Shawn thought he saw tears running down Dave's face as they drove through the night.

EPILOGUE

ALICE HYDE MEDICAL CENTER
MALONE, NEW YORK—JUNE 28, 2015

Michael McCaffrey, the man from Malone who had followed every facet of the manhunt, first hears the news via Facebook: a trooper has captured David Sweat.

"C'mon, let's go to the hospital, and maybe we can see them bring him in!" he says to his wife, Terry. Within twenty minutes they are outside Alice Hyde Medical Center, hoping to get a glimpse of the fugitive.

Soon after, an ambulance pulls in. McCaffrey holds up his camera phone and hits record. The small crowd watches as the truck backs into the emergency entrance, where state troopers and police are waiting. Cops try to push the spectators back, but McCaffrey, who bears the size and likeness of a lumberjack, stands firm.

The ambulance parks and cops help open its doors.

"Wicked, eh?!" McCaffrey says aloud.

Seconds later, paramedics unload the gurney with Sweat strapped to it and rush him inside.

"There he goes!" McCaffrey said, trying to keep the camera steady. "He's got camo on, eh? You seen it!? You seen him movin' and shit!? Awesome! I want to hear that damn story!"

TITUS MOUNTAIN SKI RESORT
MALONE, NEW YORK—JUNE 28, 2015

Members of the New York State Police, the U.S. Marshals, the Clinton County Sheriff's Department, and other law enforcement agencies stand behind Gov. Andrew Cuomo as he takes the podium at Titus Mountain Ski Resort, head-quarters for the manhunt.

"We are here with good news, as I'm sure you've heard already," he says to the crowd of officers.

"The nightmare is finally over. It took twenty-two days, but we can now confirm—as of two days ago, as you know, Mr. Matt is deceased, and the other escapee, Mr. Sweat, is [now] in custody.[40] He is in stable condition. Let's give a big round of applause to the men and women of law enforcement."

Whoops, hollers, and applause erupt from those gathered in the Upper Lodge.

"This was an extraordinary situation in many ways," he

---

40 The escape lasted twenty-three days, from June 6 through June 29, if June 29—the day Sweat was captured—is considered one full day.

continues. "The prison in Dannemora is over one hundred years old. This is the first escape in one hundred years. If you were writing a movie plot, they would say that this was overdone...

"But one escape is one escape too many. We will have the ongoing investigation to find out exactly who was involved. We have two people who have been arrested for facilitation or were accomplices in this situation, but the investigation is not over. Now that we have Mr. Sweat, it gives us the opportunity to ask some more questions and provide more facts on the overall situation. Anyone who we find who was culpable and guilty of cooperating in this escape will be fully prosecuted...

"Today ends with good news. These were really dangerous, dangerous men, both Matt and Sweat. They were killers. Mr. Matt killed at least two people. Mr. Sweat killed a sheriff's deputy in Broome County in a savage, savage way. So these were dangerous people. We could not tolerate them being on the loose...

"This was an unprecedented coming together of law enforcement on every level. We had local law enforcement, we had federal law enforcement, state assets, all working together, hand in glove, with gears meshing...

"And last but not least, I want to thank the people of the State of New York, who, as usual, stepped up to the challenge. People in Franklin County, Clinton County— they had all sorts of leads. They were on the lookout. Law enforcement didn't end here. Every citizen did their job and they did it bravely, and they did it courageously, and they dealt with the increased police presence and the fear, frankly, of having to go three weeks knowing that there were murderers loose in your backyards.

"But New Yorkers are tough and they stepped right up. They stepped up to the challenge, they provided help, and they stood with us every step of the way. I want to thank the people in Franklin and Clinton County personally for their courage and every law enforcement officer—literally thousands of law enforcement officers—were engaged in this. And it's nice when it ends well."

HAMBURG, NEW YORK—JULY 4, 2015

Fifteen people gather in a small church in Hamburg, New York, for a private funeral service for Richard Matt. A pastor from Bethesda Church in Tonawanda leads a prayer. Matt's ex-wife, Vee Marie Harris, has come, as well as their children, Francesca and Nick. Greg Durandetto is also there, accompanied by his mother, who has fond memories of Matt as a boy scoffing down spaghetti and meatballs at her dining room table.

Durandetto is among the first to speak.

"We all know the bad he did, but this is not how I remember Rick," he says. The summer heat is stifling. He wishes someone would open a window. "He did bad things, but there was good in him. I can only fill in the blanks from what I know."

His words are met with mostly silence. Durandetto had envisioned this day differently: he had seen them sharing stories of Matt's teenage years with hearty laughter. The quiet is unsettling.

He looks over at Matt's children. He had met his son a few summers back. He had not met Matt's daughter, but he knows her immediately. She looks just like her father before he turned down a dark path from which he would never truly escape.

CLINTON COUNTY COURT
PLATTSBURGH, NEW YORK—FEBRUARY 3, 2016

David Sweat takes a seat in Clinton County Court. His shaven head, wire-framed glasses, and light skin—which had not seen the sun for several months—make him look older than his thirty-five years. Thick metal links are wrapped around his waist and secured with a Master lock. His wrists are cuffed to the chain, and his ankles are shackled. Five members of the DOCCS Correctional Emergency Response Team (CERT) stand within inches of where he sits. Few others are present for the proceeding.

Judge Patrick McGill speaks first.

"This is a matter of the people of State of New York against David P. Sweat. We're here for sentencing."

Clinton County District Attorney Andrew Wylie gives a nod and begins.

"The people have reviewed the pre-sentence investigation report, Your Honor, that was prepared by Seneca County Probation Department as well as Clinton County Probation Department," he says. "On the date the defendant entered his plea, Your Honor, he entered it through a three-count indictment, which consisted of two counts of escape in the first degree and one count of promoting prison contraband in the first degree. The sentences that the court could impose in this matter is a three and a half to seven-year determinate or indeterminate sentence, Your Honor. *[sic]* Those sentences would be imposed consecutive to the life without parole sentence that Mr. Sweat is presently serving, which he received on or about September 24, 2003, which was life without parole for his conviction by pleading to murder in the first degree.

"Your Honor, we would ask the court to impose that maximum sentence upon Mr. Sweat this morning. We would also ask that you impose fines and surcharges subject to your discretion that the defendant would also be required to [give] a DNA sample...and lastly, Your Honor, the people are asking the court to order restitution in the amount of $79,841—and that is the monetary amount the New York State Department of Corrections incurred as a result of repairing the prison cell walls, the interior portions of the facility that Sweat and Matt had both destroyed as a result of their escape. It also includes the repair and replacement of the steam pipe on the inside and the outside of the facility, [the damage of] which were also caused by Sweat and Matt during the escape.

"Your Honor, this escape, in and of itself, obviously caused trauma, caused anguish, caused fear to the citizens here in Clinton County—not only in Clinton County, but Franklin County, Essex County, New York State, and probably the United States, while these two men were out for the time period between June 6 and June 28, 2015. And as a result of that, the expenses that the state incurred and that fear that was set in, I think it is very important for this court to impose the maximum sentence, even though it would be imposed on a life without parole sentence. There is really no difference in a situation like this whether the defendant is serving a life without parole sentence, whether the defendant is serving a ten-year determinate or ten to twenty-year sentence, or a five-year sentence in state prison. That [a] crime was committed, that the defendant committed that crime, the defendant admitted to committing that crime, and that a just and proper sentence needs to be imposed as a result of that. And that is one of the reasons why we prosecuted this case—to also send that message out to any inmate, whether they're at a local jail or at a state facility, that here at least in Clinton County, they will be prosecuted. Thank you."

McGill nods, then says, "Mr. Mucia?"

Sweat's court-appointed lawyer, Joe Mucia, rises to his feet.

"Thank you, Your Honor—and good morning. First, I would note that unlike Mrs. Mitchell and Mr. Palmer, my client has taken full responsibility for his actions. That at Mrs. Mitchell's sentencing, she showed very little remorse. And it should be noted that Mr. Palmer is still denying all responsibility over his role in the prison escape.

"But Mr. Sweat has taken the full responsibility by pleading guilty to the entire indictment. That is, all three counts that were lodged against him. Secondly, I would note that Mr. Sweat has cooperated with the IG's—the inspector general's office. He has provided very useful information to the inspector general's office that should be noted for the record...It should also be noted for the record that after Mr. Sweat was shot, he spoke with law enforcement agents while he was in the Albany Medical Center. Mr. Sweat revealed to those agents that there [was] a point in time when Mr. Sweat and Mr. Matt were on the lam, and Mr. Matt threatened to take hostages, to kidnap people and to kill people. And it was Mr. Sweat who talked down Mr. Matt from doing that. So I would say that Mr. Sweat saved some lives. There's another occasion when Mr. Sweat and Mr. Matt were on the lam, and Mr. Matt—he had a shotgun, he had pointed the shotgun at a law enforcement official and Mr. Matt was going to shoot that official—but Mr. Sweat stopped him from doing that...

"As far as any fines, as far as any surcharges, as far as any restitution, we would object. And the reason is Mr. Sweat is serving six years in a special housing unit—the SHU. And while he is in the SHU, he does not receive any commissary whatsoever. Once he is eligible to get out of the SHU, in six years, Mr. Sweat will be eligible for what's called grade three work. And it is my understanding, based upon the rules and regulations of the Department of Corrections, that grade three work gives Mr. Sweat six dollars per week. And it's my further understanding, based on the Department of Corrections rules and regulations, that 20 percent of that salary, so to speak, will be taken out of the six dollars per week and applied to any order of restitution or fines and surcharges. So that is $1.20 per week that will be applied to any order of restitution. So this will not be paid off. I did the math...it is 1,029 years...

"He has no resources whatsoever. Mrs. Mitchell, she has a pension, and Mr. Palmer—I believe he will be eligible for Social Security; he'll have a pension on his own. So

I believe the order of restitution is better placed on Mrs. Mitchell and Mr. Palmer.

"Lastly, what I would note is, I have spoken to my client. He is remorseful. He does apologize for his role in the prison escape. He apologizes for the trauma and for the fear that he put on the state of New York in the County of Clinton. That's all I have to say—Mr. Sweat may want to say something."

McGill steps down from the bench.

"Mr. Sweat?" says McGill.

Sweat stands. The place is silent. He chooses his words carefully, he will later say, hoping not to make a fool of himself.

"Yes, Your Honor." His voice is soft but he speaks with conviction. "I would like to apologize to the community and people who felt fear and felt it necessary to you know, leave their homes or community because of the escape. That was never my intent and I deeply apologize for that, Your Honor."

He remains standing, waiting for the judge.

"The court has read the presentencing report," McGill says. "I thank the Seneca County Probation Department for putting together a report that gives some insight, I believe, into this situation.

"For approximately a month or so, this community was in turmoil. A number of people were exposed to danger. The officers and correction officers were placed in harm's way because of Mr. Sweat's actions. It's evident to me, from reading the report, that Mr. Sweat is not stupid. He is intelligent, articulate, and understands what has happened to him and what he's done.

"He has, however, made stupid choices, beginning

very early in his life, in 1993 to the present. One of his more stupid decisions was [being] convicted of murder in 2002...When he [first] joined forces with Mr. Matt to try and escape from Clinton Correctional Facility—[this] was another stupid decision...I know what you're thinking presently, but I don't know what you're thinking at the time. I find it difficult to contemplate that you felt escape would allow you to resume the freedom that you once enjoyed.

"If you think that there would not be an all-out effort to bring you back into custody, I think it was another stupid decision—one that struck fear into the community that it didn't deserve, one that extended vast amounts of resources...one that put hundreds of men and women in harm's way, and one that put you in the hospital with injuries you are still struggling with, one that killed a fellow inmate. How would you term it other than stupid?

"You seem to indicate that you tried to escape to show the shortcomings of the correctional system or as a protest of treatment received from correction officers. Aside from the organizing an escape, I would ask, did you do anything to bring about change in the facility? Organizing, or complaining, or lodging complaints with regard to treatment or decisions made in the correctional facility? Maybe if you had expended the energy you expended in escaping to reform the programs and conditions in the prison, you might have changed the outcome...

"Sentencing you is anticlimatical [sic] since life without parole, as they say, is what it is..."

"For acts there are consequences, and unfortunately, you have had consequences a plenty."

• • •

CONKLIN, NEW YORK—FEBRUARY 28, 2016

Pamela Sweat stands at the top of her trailer stoop, her bare arms crossed, the bulk of her ample body blocking the front door. Her posture matches her countenance, which resembles that of a bulldog. The weight of her jowls deepens the folds of her rather broad face, which, with its heavy brow and handsome nose, is the last visible remnant of her Cherokee bloodline.

Nearly eight months have passed since law enforcement apprehended her son after his breakout from Clinton Correctional Facility. The way Pamela sees it, the only upside to the escape was his transfer to a closer prison. The ninety-mile drive from her mobile home in Conklin to upstate Romulus beat the three-hundred-mile journey to Dannemora; she had rarely visited her youngest child before 2015, as long car rides exacerbated her arthritis and diabetes, which had set in by age fifty-nine. But, she says, even the shorter, two-hour road trip to Five Points Correctional Facility gives her trouble. To see her son, Pamela first asks her friend Carol or daughter Anna for a lift. The second option always requires a babysitter for Anna's children, a task usually left to Sweat's estranged eldest sister, Matilda, who loathes her brother. If Tilly Tuttle—the last name Matilda prefers, taken from their mother's side—agrees to look after Anna's kids, Pamela and Anna are then free to drive to Five Points.

Visitation day unfolds like this: they arrive at the facility before 8 a.m., always among the first in line for security. To speed up the process, Pamela brings only the essentials—a photo ID and a clear sandwich bag full of quarters to buy lunch, usually pre-cooked, plastic-wrapped cheeseburgers and chicken wings from visitor vending machines. (The mid-morning meal often puts her right to sleep.)

"I've been up to see him about three times...They wouldn't let me see him for two months after he got put away, 'cause he had to be by himself," she says, speaking in a backwoods twang. "I was just there last weekend. I've got to save up to go back. I usually give him fifty dollars. Not easy gettin', but I get it. David said it's better than the food that's in there. He said, 'That food's nasty, Ma! Be sure to bring lots of change.'"

"He's real skinny now, hardly don't look like David, being up in the woods for three weeks and all. He said they're finally going to do something with his shoulder. I said, well, I hope so. The gunshot, that took his shoulder right out. He called a new doctor and I guess he said they have to do it. That's what he said, the lawyer told him they're required to fix it 'cause they're the ones that did it even though he ran away. Well we don't really talk about what he did. It's good he don't. He said he don't want to 'cause he don't want me into it, 'cause I have bipolar, so he doesn't want me getting into it. I said, 'Well you shoulda' stayed where you were.'"

Pam's fingers suddenly dig into the flesh of her right arm. "When I go like this and stuff I get nervous," she says. "Getting an anxiety attack."

Maturity and medications now help stabilize the unpredictable mood swings that had plagued most of her adolescence. "That's all I got all my life—people telling me I'm stupid," she says of her days at Greene High School, when her manic episodes brought on ridicule from her classmates. "I'd go home and punch the hell out of my pillow. My brother Jimmy said, 'Sissy, don't worry about it. Laugh it off.'" But Pamela says being placed in a class for students with learning disabilities was hard to laugh off. At sixteen, after one particular row with her teacher, Pamela recalls asking the instructor, "Will I ever get a diploma and make something of my life?" to which, as she remembers it, the woman replied, "No, that's why you're in special ed." So, she simply dropped out.

Around this time, she took up with her teenage sweetheart, Donnie Paul Sweat. "You promised me when you were thirteen you'd die a Sweat," he had once told her. After one child—Matilda—and two years of marriage, the couple permanently parted ways, though she neither legally divorced Donnie nor dropped the surname. She would give that name to her future offspring, Anna and David Paul, whom she had with a man named Floyd Kenyon.

Of the three, she says it is David who tested her patience the most.

"Sometimes he's too smart for his own britches. [When he was little] his adventure was going through the gardens, finding toys, bringing them home, fixing them up. He got a VHS that wasn't working, he took it apart, put a big thick rubber band on there and it worked fine. That's just the way he was. But he was a handful. He used to get mad and punch the wall and knock down a shelf, and got mad at me and pulled the bathroom door off."

"A lot of people where he is at [now] said they would rather have him where he is now 'cause they know he can't get out of that one like he did the other one. Last year, I was planning on going up to see him. June the fourteenth was our birthday. He took off the sixth. I was so upset I cried. I couldn't go to sleep. I couldn't eat, especially when I heard how many times they shot that other guy in the head."

CLINTON COUNTY COURT
PLATTSBURGH, NEW YORK—FEBRUARY 29, 2016

Standing in a gray suit and red tie next to his lawyer William Dreyer, an attorney brought in from Albany to handle his case, Gene Palmer says the word "guilty" three times—once for promoting prison contraband in the second degree, once for promoting prison contraband in the first degree, and once for official misconduct. After nine months of negotiations with the Clinton County District Attorney's Office and the court, the charges of tampering with evidence are dropped.[41] A $5,000 fine is imposed, as well as a $375 courtroom surcharge. Palmer retires from his position as a corrections officer, where he had earned $74,644 base salary.

"Mr. Palmer had no idea that he was knowingly aiding anybody to escape, [it's] the last thing he ever thought of, that there would be an escape at Dannemora," Dreyer tells the court.

District Attorney Andrew Wylie disagrees.

"I think he needs to be incarcerated, whether the court deems that to be a state prison sentence or a, say, one-year term in county jail," he says.

Judge Kevin Ryan opts to hand Palmer a six-month sentence in Clinton County Jail.

---

41 The tampering with evidence charge related to allegations that Palmer had burned the paintings Matt had given him.

"The introduction of the screwdriver and pliers into the facility have the potential of actually making the facility less safe, not more," he says. "[But] sending a [corrections] officer to state prison as an inmate would create a monumental challenge for the prison."

In light of Palmer's sentencing, New York State Inspector General Catherine Leahy Scott issues the following statement:

> "This disgraced corrections officer's disregard for the laws and rules guiding his profession underscores his criminal culpability in the systemic breakdown of security that led to last summer's escape of two convicted killers. His actions made him a key enabler for the convicts' escape plans and helped illuminate many of the procedural failures throughout Clinton Correctional Facility that I have been thoroughly investigating to help make sure it never happens again."

FIVE POINTS CORRECTIONAL FACILITY ROMULUS, NEW YORK—MARCH 6, 2016

Sweat has spent most of his eight months at Five Points Correctional Facility alone in "the box." The guards have switched his cell several times since he first arrived, but the rooms—all part of the prison's Solitary Housing Unit, each complete with a shower, twin bed, toilet, and a shelf, where Sweat keeps a tidy row of books—look more or less the same. Here, he passes the time reading (recently, *A Walk in the Woods: Rediscovering America on the Appalachian Trail* by Bill Bryson disappointed him because the protagonists did not complete the entire 2,000-mile trek) or writing letters to his mother, Pamela, his sister, Anna, and to his teenage son, Bradly, whom he has not seen in more than ten years. Mealtimes break up the monotony, yet he rarely looks forward to the dishes they slide under his door, mostly things like limp pasta and bland potatoes.

His green uniform hangs loosely on his frame. He had once squatted five hundred pounds of metal in Clinton's yard; now he struggles to complete a single pushup. His right arm is propped at an angle, suspended by a blue sling with a white strap. A surgeon has yet to weld the loose fragments of his cracked collar bone, which, when he tugs the neckline of his shirt and shrugs his shoulder, shift beneath the flesh in an unnatural way.

He recalls the moments after his bones were shattered in amazing detail:

> *Sweat looked and saw that he was handcuffed. He did not remember the restraints being put on.*
>
> *"I need to lean over and spit," he had said.*
>
> *"Don't spit on me!" said one of the troopers.*
>
> *He was propped up. He felt his conscious beginning to slip. He felt his body begin to shut down.*
>
> *"I don't think I'm going to make it."*
>
> *"He should've killed you," said another voice.*
>
> *"Don't let him bleed out," said Cook. "We need the intel."*
>
> *A third cop knelt down on his left. Sweat could feel the pressure of fingers on his wound to keep his blood from spilling out.*

"Hold on, David. Just hold on."
Everything went dark.

Sweat looks down at the sling cradling his right arm. He now knows what he looked like that day in the alfalfa field: a friend had sent him one of the few images taken shortly after his capture. The photo shows him in camo pants with three state troopers standing around him in a circle. He keeps this picture in an envelope near his bed.

"That cop behind me, he had his knee in my back. He acted like he didn't want to touch me," Sweat says in seat C7 in the Five Points visitation room. Guards walk past as he speaks. His voice is faint from lack of use.

"It looks like a hunting photo, only I'm the deer. I guess they got their big white buck."

Memories of what happened next come in flashes. There was the ambulance ride. Medics cut his pants off and clipped his necklace. The driver sped along a dirt road. Someone next to him, an EMT he thinks, called out for them to slow down. A woman prodded at his right shin, which hurt like hell.

Sweat arrived at Alice Hyde Medical Center. Nurses bustled past his hospital bed. He heard the beeps of the heart monitor. An oxygen mask covered his nose and mouth. He asked a doctor to remove the sock on his left foot. A cop, he thinks, took it for evidence.

When he woke up again, he was in Albany Medical Center. His wrists and ankles had been chained to the bed. CERT officers from DOCCS stood outside his door. Nurses came in to feed him. Of them, his favorite had been Daphne, a soft, bubbly woman with hazelnut skin. She was there when the investigators first arrived to question him about the escape.

A week later, at 3:05 a.m., officers wheeled him out the back door of the hospital. They loaded him into a vehicle flanked by police escorts and brought him to an airport in Albany, where they waited for the fog to lift before flying to Five Points Correctional Facility.

Once at the prison, he had been photographed and brought into a cell in the infirmary. A CO sat outside his door twenty-four hours a day. They had been prepared to place him on suicide watch.

Sweat has had many close calls in life. He has crashed a four wheeler, fallen out of a tree, and had a van drop right on him while working as a mechanic. Each time he walks away, mostly unscathed.

"I always say I took a bullet to break a bone—and I don't count this!" He points to the slight bump in his nose, the result of a water polo injury in high school.

"I'm lucky," he says with a smile. "Like a bastard."

Being shot was not the way Sweat wanted to end his "three-week vacation," as he now calls it. He had envisioned a home near the water, one he'd build himself, perhaps a door down from his friend, Richard Matt.

Sweat knows his friend was responsible for his own fate. An autopsy revealed that Matt's blood alcohol content was .18 percent—more than twice the national legal limit for operating a motor vehicle. He was the one who had chosen to drink, and he had left Sweat no choice.

"If I hadn't left him, he would probably still be alive," he says. "I had to accept it. I couldn't dwell on it. Because of the way I grew up, I have to accept things for what they are."

These facts, however, give him little comfort now as he thinks back to the day Matt handed him a silver dollar at Twisted Horn, hours before the manhunt took a turn that would permanently seal their fate.

Sweat's only solace is that he helped his friend, the Midnight Rider, get his one final wish.

"Matt didn't want to die in prison," he says. "He just wanted to die free. So in a way, he got what he wanted—it's what he would've wanted. I didn't want to die. I wanted to live free. It's a waste of life being in here. No one should spend the rest of his life in prison."

Sweat looks around the Five Points visitation room. Rows of long tables and lacquered benches fill the space. The main area is divided by windowless, bar-less partitions. In the back of the room there's more secluded seating, reserved for the prison's more "problematic" inmates. Nearby, visitors bustle from one vending machine to another, surveying the selection of chips, sodas and pre-cooked meals as microwaves hum, warming the cellophane-wrapped turkey and Swiss sandwiches and meatball subs.

He peers out into the sea of green shirts. Freedom, he says, is on the minds of all incarcerated men.

"If they tell you they're not thinking about it," he says, "they're shitting you."

NEW YORK STATE POLICE BARRACKS MALONE, NEW YORK—MARCH 24, 2017

The wall behind Sgt. Cook's desk is covered in awards,

hung up by his colleagues at the Malone Barracks. There's the superintendent's commendation for "outstanding performance of duty and exceptional contribution to the New York State Police," the 2016 Top Cop recognition from the National Association of Police Organizations, resolutions from the Franklin County Legislature and the New York State Legislature to thank him for protecting the public, the Officer of the Month Award from the National Law Enforcement Officers Memorial Fund. In the middle of these accolades is a metal sign: "Began on Cook Ended with Cook."[42]

When he retires, the certificates, laques, and other things he received for capturing Sweat will most likely go in a box.

"I have deer heads in my house," Cook says with a wry smile. "They wouldn't fit in."

The idea that he's "a hero" doesn't sit well with the sergeant. He is a soft-spoken man with a dignified presence who is well-known and well-liked, yet considers himself "just an average guy who grew up on a farm and makes syrup."

Yet that day in the alfalfa field left a permanent mark on Cook, who recalls the event and the hour after with startling clarity:

> *"You all right?" said Senior Investigator Kurt Taylor.*
> *They stood several feet from where Sweat was being*
> *treated for the bullet wounds.*
> *"Yeah, I think so," said Cook.*
> *"How many times did you shoot?"*

---

42 The sign is reference to Cook's name and Cook Street in Dannemora, where the prison is located.

"I think twice."

"Where were ya?"

The sergeant looked over and saw Sweat's bag.

"Right there by that backpack somewhere," he said, pointing.

Taylor looked in the direction of the bag, then towards Sweat. An investigator who had inspected the inmate's tattoos gave Taylor the thumbs up. The markings matched. They had their guy.

Taylor turned back to Cook.

"I'm going to need your gun," he said. The weapon was now part of the investigation into the escape.

"Yeah, I know."

The sergeant pulled out his .45 GAP and handed it over. But Taylor would not let the sergeant go unarmed. He handed Cook his own weapon, which he readily holstered.

"C'mon," the investigator said. "Let's go."

Halfway to the patrol car, Cook felt his stomach churn.

"I've got to stop for a second." His face was clammy. His head was light. He bent over, ready to hurl.

A few seconds passed. Then, the spell subsided.

When he reached the patrol car, a lieutenant approached him.

"You all right? You should go to the hospital."

"No, I don't need to go to the hospital," he said. "I'll be fine."

Back at the barracks that day, Maj. Charles E. Guess had joined his wife, the captains, and other officers in

Troop B to congratulate the sergeant. Gov. Andrew Cuomo had paid him a phone call. Hundreds of emails—some offering praise, others requesting interviews—had flooded his inbox. His phone had blown up with text messages. The media had already swarmed his house, a quaint, white, well-kept ranch on a dead-end street surrounded by maple trees. A trooper was posted outside of his home for one week to keep the press at bay.

By Wednesday—three days after the shooting—Cook returned to work.

"I could've taken off as long as I wanted," he says. "But just sitting home was not helping. I wanted to get back."

"The emotions that went through me after my encounter with him—it's very hard to explain. It still runs through your head. It's really weird to talk about. It doesn't feel sometimes like it happened. I still don't sleep well at night. I was never a good sleeper anyway but boy, the months following I had a real tough time sleeping. Shit would run through your head constantly. I didn't feel bad about it. I don't know, it was just out of the norm. That could've went so many different frickin' ways. I could've been the one who let him get away.

"Sweat, in my opinion, was very young when he did what he did. He was into some bad shit with the burglaries and stuff. But that night they killed Kevin Tarsia…now he's paying the whole rest of his life for what he did. I have no sympathy."

ALBANY, NEW YORK—JUNE 6, 2016

One year after the escape out of Clinton Correctional

Facility, the State of New York Office of the Inspector General put out a 150-page report of findings from its investigation.

It concluded:

> "The June 5 escape from Clinton was planned and executed by two particularly cunning and resourceful inmates, abetted by the willful, criminal conduct of a civilian employee of the prison's tailor shops, and assisted by the reckless actions of a veteran correction officer. The escape could not have occurred, however, except for longstanding breakdowns in basic security functions at Clinton and DOCCS executive management's failure to identify and correct these deficiencies...
>
> "Significantly, the many failures revealed by the inspector general's investigation did not arise only as Sweat and Matt planned and executed their escape. Indeed, they are of long duration and reflect a complacency regarding security at Clinton that is alarming and unacceptable. One DOCCS executive testified that basic security practices at Clinton were characterized by a "culture of carelessness." The inspector general is incredulous that high ranking security staff, including executive management officials, were unaware of these deficient practices."

The search cost the state approximately $23 million in state law enforcement overtime alone. Additional costs included those incurred by other local, state, and federal agencies, as well as $573,000 on extra security and repairs to the prison.[43]

A wave of suspensions, reassignments, and resignations followed. Within ten months, sixty-four Clinton workers retired from the DOCCS—67 percent more than during the same time period the year before. Many COs did not want to deal with the policy changes implemented at the prison post-escape, some would later say, while others did not want to be seen as connected to the dirty dealings behind the white wall.

By the fall of 2016, a wave of new recruits arrived at the prison. Along Cook Street, each light pole was flying a red, white, and blue pennant flag bearing the words, "Clinton Strong."

FIVE POINTS CORRECTIONAL FACILITY ROMULUS, NEW YORK—MARCH 20, 2016

Sweat often thinks of his son, Bradly. Occasionally he receives a letter from the boy, now a teenager with his father's physique. Sweat knows April had married a man named Bill, an aircraft mechanic. "That was a good pick," he says, giving one thumb up. He wants someone bright to teach his son.

A few years back, Bradly wrote Sweat a letter that said he and his dad went fishing. But the boy had scratched out "dad" and in the small space above scribbled the word "Bill."

---

43 Statistics are taken from the June 2016 report released by the State of New York Office of the Inspector General.

"I wrote him back," Sweat says. "I told him—he raised you. He was there for all of the big moments. Don't you feel bad about calling him that. Bill deserves to be called dad."

He is silent for a minute before speaking again in the Five Points visitation room. This time, he brings up Bradly's mother, April.

"It was too hard on her, all of this," he says, indicating the steel doors and other inmates. They had tried to stay together for a few years after he was locked up, but being separated by concrete and barbed wire eventually took its toll.

"I can understand," he says.

Sweat thinks back to a day some fifteen years before, when he and April had sat on the edge of a dock to watch the sun rise.

"It's about to get sappy," a younger Sweat had thought. He had begun to fidget. He had cracked a joke. The joke had offended April.

"You always ruin these moments," she had said to him.

His eyes begin to well up.

"I ruin a lot of moments."

A few minutes later, a familiar voice calls out from two seats away.

"That's Sweat! He taught me how to sew! Hey, Sweat!"

Tyrone, a tall, brawny inmate with dark skin and thick black frames, who is also relegated to SHU, has not seen his Industry teacher for at least two years, since they last worked together in Clinton's tailor shop. They both sit on circular metal stools on the same side of a long table with steel partitions, facing their visitors. Tyrone is across from a smartly dressed woman and a baby girl named Sojourn, who giggles and taps her feet playfully as her mother lifts her from the bench and props her up on the table.

"Hey Sweat, you still paintin'?" He says this just loud enough for the words to carry. The COs do not like it when the inmates, especially those in SHU, speak to one another during visitation. "They probably don't give you any brushes."

Sweat shakes his head.

"I'm not doing much of anything," he says.

A bit later, Tyrone calls out to one of the guards to request a bathroom break. He stands up and walks a few feet. As he waits for the CO, he turns back to Sweat.

"They shot you in the back!?" His wide eyes rove to the sling.

Sweat nods.

"Man!" says Tyrone. "When you and Hacksaw were out there, I was like, 'Yeah, they did it! They gonna make it!' Couldn't think of two better guys to do it. I watched the news, anytime I could get my hands on a newspaper or something I would. Then they killed Hacksaw. Man, that's rough. How long they give you for that?"

"Six years." He speaks quietly, but not out of concern for the COs.

Tyrone looks down in disbelief.

"Six years?! Man, that's a long time."

BINGHAMTON, NEW YORK—JULY 24, 2016

Shawn Devaul sits at a wooden picnic table in the shade of Rec Park, the whimsical chords of Binghamton's historic carousel humming in the background. His light skin is decorated with several tattoos, the most noticeable being the large gray skull on his right calf. Black socks, camo shorts, and thick, dark boots heighten the contrast, as does the black t-shirt with the word NOMAD printed in bold lettering inspired by the Middle Ages.

Devaul, now thirty-seven, has tried to keep a low profile over the last thirteen years. He does not tell people where he lives, where he works, or that he ever did three years behind bars for his role in the shooting that sent Sweat to Clinton. Yet privately, Devaul followed every twist and turn of the manhunt, keeping tabs on the man with whom he would always be inextricably linked.

"That cop [Cook] is lucky he decided to take the shots because he wouldn't have caught him [on foot]," he says. "I tried racing him before, and I used to be fast. He was faster than me; he was like a track star. That's why I say if they wouldn't have took the shots, he would've been gone; that tree line was only a few more feet away. He would've been running in the woods still 'cause he's quick like that. He was a fast mother. I mean, he's fast."

His words drift off as do his thoughts, floating from memory to memory. He talks of Sweat doing mechanical work on his car, their hangouts in the den on Dickinson Street, their time on One Dirt Road.

Devaul admits he was never close to Sweat. Yet now he sees a very different man than the one he remembers from their days back in Binghamton.

"Just looking at his face it almost seems like he's broken," Devaul says, recalling photos and video clips of Sweat he had seen circulating in the media.

"He's not a monster or anything that what people

would call somebody that killed somebody. It's not in him no more. I don't know if it ever was in him, really."

FIVE POINTS CORRECTIONAL FACILITY
ROMULUS, NEW YORK—JULY 23, 2016

In 2010 Sweat received a letter from Julia Hunter, a reporter from the *Press & Sun-Bulletin*. It had been eight years since the death of Sheriff's Deputy Kevin Tarsia, and she wanted his comment for a story.

On May 29, 2010, Sweat wrote her the following response:

> "I received your letter yesterday on the 28th. I really appreciate the opportunity to tell my side of the story. I have given it alot of thought and don't see how any thing positive could come of it for anyone and may just have an adverse affect by bringing up something many people affected by what happened have been trying to deal with or move on from, in their own ways. So I must respectfuly decline. I do how ever wish you luck in writing the story because Im sure your editor intends for you to do so regardless. In doing so I hope that you will keep in mind and be compassionate to all the people and familys involved and affected by (as you put it) the events that led to my incarceration. As far as how I am doing, if it were a personal question, but I believe you are simply writing as a reporter which to me means

anything I write is subjectable to interpretation and may or may not be wrote as a whole. Besides, its prison, how could a person realy be doing :)

"Well, Kentucky :) I do thank you for your time and consideration. Sorry I cant help but good luck with the new job at the Press & Sun-Bulletin!"

In an interview earlier that month, Inspector General Catherine Leahy-Scott said Sweat would grow agitated when they asked him questions that might tarnish his reputation, calling him "very smart, very cunning, very narcissistic."

"She said I thought, I always thought, I was the smartest guy in the room," says Sweat. This time he's in Legal Room A1, an enclosed space walled in by thick panes of glass and a heavy steel door just large enough to fit a desk-sized table and three plastic chairs, if three slender visitors squeeze together. (The guards have placed more restrictions on his visits, and he is no longer permitted to sit among the other SHU inmates. There is no real reason for this relegation, he says.)

"Well that's just not true," he continues. "I don't know who the smartest guy in the room is because I might not know everyone in the room. I could be in a room full of people and one of them could be some scientist who has discovered something I know nothing about. And a narcissist doesn't have compassion."

TAYLORSVILLE, NORTH CAROLINA —AUGUST 10, 2016

Floyd Kenyon sits at his small kitchen table in Taylorsville,

North Carolina, a clear flexible tube connecting his nostrils to a nearby oxygen tank. The device is a relatively new addition to the one-bedroom apartment on Zion Avenue, as his worsening chronic obstructive pulmonary disease (COPD)—stemming from coal workers' pneumoconiosis, or "black lung"—causes him to wheeze with every breath. At sixty-one, Kenyon spends the better part of his days tending to this ailment as well as a lengthy list of other conditions, including diabetes and congestive heart failure. Every three hours or so, Kenyon tests his blood sugar, and, with precise penmanship, neatly jots down the number in a ruled notebook, a ritual of orderliness in which he takes a certain amount of pride. He applies the same sense of organization to his home; in his kitchenette, a series of plastic and wooden spoons, spatulas, and ladles hang along the backsplash in descending order of size, and, a few feet away, piles of papers sit in tidy stacks on a card table. Even the art on his walls—a painting of a Native American man in a feathered war bonnet, a poster-size print of the Twin Towers, a headshot of country singer Sonny James, a needlepoint of a handsome buck, a portrait of the Virgin Mary—are hung with great care and forethought.

Near the front door hangs another picture, a black-and-white photograph of his father's farm that once sat on 180 acres of land in upstate New York in the town Smithville Flats.

"I could remember when I had to get up at three o'clock in the morning, get the cows, move 'em to the barn, get 'em all cleaned up and then get ready for school." He looks at the photograph as he says the words, which come out with a slight lisp and a wheeze, the result of his COPD and several missing teeth. "I miss the country. Be nice to be back. Be a lot better to get out of this apartment."

Kenyon fondly recalls his days at Greene High School, where he first met Pamela Sweat—a "nice" underclassman and the sister of his friend, Jim Tuttle. The two had quickly taken to one another and, within five years of an on-again, off-again romance, the couple gave birth to a daughter named Anna, and, soon after, to a son named David. Their relationship, however, would not last long; within two years of David's birth in Binghamton, the couple split.

"She wanted to do it her way and I said, 'That's what you wanna do, then I'll go my way.' And that's the way we went…Last time I saw [David] he was in court, Family Court, him and Anna, I seen both of them at the same time. Last time I ever saw him he was real young. Been a long time…Off and on [I] thought about them. I just wondered where they were. Now I'm missing nobody. You see what I'm getting at. The way I look at it, they is thinkin' I don't exist."

He pauses to inhale. The air rattles as it fills his lungs.

"I blame them anyhow 'cause none of them keep in touch with me or nothin'. Sometimes I wish I was in touch with them. The way I look at it, I don't exist to them. The way I look at it, it's a long road for them. What goes around comes around."

The next time Kenyon saw his son's face was on the evening news in the summer of 2015.

"I didn't know that was him. That kind of caught me off guard. I didn't know about it until the officers came," he says, remembering the day when law enforcement questioned him on his son's whereabouts.

"The officer told me about it and I was like, 'What? You've got to be kidding me.' I says I don't know nothing about it and didn't wanna know nothing about it. I didn't want ta' get involved. The way I look at it, Dave was wrong. Let him suffer with it…He's got to pay the price. You do the crime, you got to do your time. That's the way I look at it."

Kenyon says he knew something about "doing time" after completing his own ninety-day stint in Iredell County Detention Center in Statesville, North Carolina. Six years after he parted ways with Pamela, Kenyon married a woman named Teresa, and within a year the couple had a baby girl, Peggy Mae. The family moved to Statesville, where Kenyon took a job at a sawmill in neighboring Unionville. They lived a normal working-class life, Kenyon says, until July 2001, when then fourteen-year-old Peggy Mae told authorities her father had exposed himself to her while he stood naked in the shower. In April of 2002, he pleaded guilty to five counts of "indecent liberty with a minor, sexual arousal with a child."

It was not the first time he had been accused of inappropriately touching a child. Pamela Sweat's daughter Tilly Tuttle had told her mother that Kenyon had sexually assaulted her as a teenager.[44]

"I've been down what they call a long road, what they call the hell road," Kenyon says now. "It takes a lot to come back…You've gotta work your way out of it. I have the last fourteen years since my daughter [Peggy Mae] put me behind bars, when I lost everything Iredell County Detention Center my guns and all of that. That's what hurt

---

44 Kenyon was never charged or taken to court for the allegations that he molested Tilly Tuttle.

me the most, 'cause I had a gun handed down from my dad [and] a few other stuff like that. I had toys when I was a kid, like little cars, and I lost everything."

"See," he says, looking around at the possessions in his living room. "I worked my way back."

FIVE POINTS CORRECTIONAL FACILITY ROMULUS, NEW YORK—MAY 20, 2017

During pre-trial preparations in the murder case of Broome County Sheriff's Deputy Kevin Tarsia, defense attorneys raised questions as to whether the cop died from the bullets from Sweat or the two bullets Jeffrey Nabinger later fired. If the case had gone to trial, Sweat's defense would have rested on one premise: Tarsia might have lived if not for Nabinger's point-blank shots to the head.[45]

The case never reached a jury.

"This lawyer told me that if I went to trial, I would get the death penalty," Sweat says.[46]

---

45 Sweat and his attorneys maintained that the shots Sweat fired would have been non-fatal, noting that the majority struck Tarsia's bullet-proof vest or missed completely. Preliminary findings by Broome County Coroner Dr. Timothy Jones, who was at the scene, noted that it appeared Tarsia had been shot in the head, according to a July 6, 2002 report from the *Press & Sun-Bulletin*. Findings from the official autopsy, performed at Albany Medical Center, are part of a sealed file on the case. The file was sealed following the 2015 escape from Clinton Correctional Facility, according to a spokesperson for Broome County Supreme Court. Multiple requests by the author to review the file—even in its redacted form—were repeatedly denied.
46 The State of New York reinstated capital punishment in 1995. It was abolished in 2007.

Despite a push for the death penalty by Tarsia's family, the Broome County district attorney agreed to a plea deal. Sweat and Nabinger both pleaded guilty to one count of first-degree murder that carried a life sentence with no chance of parole.

In the years since, Sweat sometimes thinks about how his life might have turned out differently. If his mother had stayed in Deposit, he might never have encountered a predator like Paul. If he had had a father and if his mother had been in better health, he might have had been spared from a life of group homes and foster care. If he and April had never moved in with Nabinger, he might not have embraced a life of crime.

These experiences, he says, will never excuse his actions on July 4, 2002. While he still believes his shots alone would not have resulted in Tarsia's death, he takes responsibility for the fact that he was present, that he ever went out that night, that he partook in something that ended in a man's murder.

"In a way, it didn't really matter if it was Jeff's shot that killed him," he says. "I should not have been there. I had a part in it. I was responsible."

BEDFORD HILLS CORRECTIONAL FACILITY
BEDFORD HILLS, NEW YORK—OCTOBER 13, 2016

Joyce Mitchell sits at a narrow table in the visitation room of Bedford Hills Correctional Facility in Westchester, an all-female maximum-security prison less than fifty miles north of Manhattan.

She thinks back to the day of her sentencing on Sept. 28, 2015, and the words she said before Judge Kevin Ryan in Clinton County Court:

> "Please allow me to start by saying how sorry I am, how much remorse I have for everything that—I'm sorry."

She lifted her cuffed hands to wipe the tears from behind her glasses before continuing to read from the speech she had written.

> "—that has happened with my part in Matt and Sweat's—I'm sorry, I'm sorry Your Honor." (More uncontrollable tears.)

> "—in Matt and Sweat's escape. If I could take it all back, I would. I can't begin to explain how sorry I am for all this, to the community, to my co-workers, to my family, to all the families of fellow officers that were involved in having to be taken away from their families in this search while these two men were on the loose.

> "I never intended for any of this to happen. As hard as it was to come forward, I knew I had to. I was raised to tell the truth. I know I didn't come out first and be completely honest, but I did bring myself to the state police and tried to help as much as I could. I'm afraid it didn't help though, but I knew it was the right thing to do.

> "I am fifty-one years old, and this is by far the worst mistake I have ever made in my life. I live with regret every day and will for the rest of my life. I've never been so disappointed in myself.

I not only let myself down but my family. My husband and my children are my life, my world, my purpose.

"I was fearful of Mr. Matt threatening to kill my husband and wanting to know where my son and my mother lived. I could not let anything happen to my husband and family. I love them all so much. I love them more than life itself, your honor.

"I'm not a bad person. I clearly made a horrible mistake. I realize I need to be responsible for my actions. But I am hoping you will have mercy on me, Your Honor. No words can explain how deeply sorry I am. I am very fearful of the consequences I'm facing, as should I be. Please know that I am seeking mental health and counseling to help me understand my actions—how my actions affected the community, my family, myself, and all who were involved.

"Why I did what I did I shall not know other than I was scared for my husband and family's lives. I know I should've told someone, but Mr. Matt had others watching and reporting to him about where and what myself and my husband were doing at all times. This is something I will never forget nor forgive myself for. Please understand that I acknowledge my actions, and I'm still trying to understand why I made the choices I did.

"I hope one day everyone involved can find it within themselves to forgive me. If not, I understand. But most importantly, I want to make it home to my family—as I fear I won't because of my actions. I'm hoping you understand how remorseful and sorry I am. None of this was ever my intention, Your Honor. Thank you for your time and consideration."

She looked up from the paper.

"Your Honor, I would wear an ankle bracelet and stay out of jail for the rest of my life if I could just go home to my family."

Her letter did little to sway the judge. Ryan told Joyce she had done "terrible things" and her actions had cost the state millions. He sentenced her to an indeterminate period of incarceration of two and one third years to seven years for promoting prison contraband in the first degree. He also sentenced her to a definite term of one year for criminal facilitation in the fourth degree. He fined her a total of $6,000 in addition to the $375 courtroom surcharge.

She now feels the court showed Palmer preferential treatment because he was a corrections officer, "a boy in blue."

In the thirteen months she has spent behind bars, Joyce has dropped a considerable amount of weight, and her hair appears to have thinned. The one thing she looks forward to is a visit from Lyle, who has since resigned from his industrial position at the prison and makes the 300-mile drive from Dickinson Center every two weeks. Joyce and Lyle talk about their children and grandchildren as they used to on those morning drives to Dannemora—except now they no longer ride anywhere together.

Joyce says her life at Clinton feels somewhat like a

distant dream. Yet when she thinks back to those days in the tailor shop, she remembers the faces of the inmates she worked with side by side—particularly one face she now associates with a heavy burden of guilt.

"I've been on both sides of it. They used to look at me and say, 'You can't imagine what it's like. At the end of the day you get to go home.' They were right. You can't imagine."

"I feel responsible for where Sweat is now. I feel so much remorse for what this has done to my family and for what this has done to him. His situation is much worse because of me. I'm in here paying the price for what I did. But I'm fortunate. I have a husband who loves me. Eventually I'll get to go home. He'll never have that. He'll never go home."

FIVE POINTS CORRECTIONAL FACILITY ROMULUS, NEW YORK—MAY 21, 2016

Sweat sits in Legal Room A1. It is not much bigger than his cell, where he spends twenty-four hours a day looking east out at the grounds of the former Seneca Army Depot—a storied patch of land that once served as a secret storage place for America's stockpile of nuclear weapons. The grounds are also part of the Finger Lakes, a lush region on the east side of New York, home to bountiful vineyards, woods, and wildlife.

"I see a lot of geese. There are so many birds around here," Sweat says, his voice brightening. "The other day I heard the loudest sound, and after my heart came back into my chest, I realized it came from this little robin on the window. I couldn't believe how close he got."

Observing nature, he says, removes him from his present reality: a long sentence of solitary confinement.

"I try not to think about it," he says. "It's better to think about now then to think about the future, like what will I eat for dinner. I can't wait until the doctor says I can work out. That will take up about two to three hours of the day."

Earlier that month, he had spoken to the deputy of security at Five Points. Sweat told him he hoped there might be a way to reduce his time in the box.

"He told me, 'Hope is a dangerous thing.' That's what he said. I couldn't believe it. All you have in here is hope."

Sweat says he's always been one to accept things for what they were. He accepts that his mother was bipolar, that his father had abandoned them, that Paul had molested him in the apartment next door to his. He accepts that he had bounced around through foster care and group homes. He has made peace, for the most part, with the events that landed him behind bars. He has come to terms with nearly everything—save for a life sentence in Clinton Correctional Facility.

"Everybody always asks me how I did it, but not why," he says. Sweat has received dozens of letters from newspapers, magazines, and television networks across the country, all looking to snag an interview. They all want to know more about the logistics. No one, he says, has asked him why he did what he did.

"Sure, there was the COs and all of those problems.

And there are a lot of them. But I can't blame it all on them. Who wants to spend their life in here? I didn't do it to be famous. I did it to get out of this madness. I wanted to start a new life. That stuff with Jeff, we did that out of ignorance. Matt and I had a cause. This had a purpose. This was about freedom. Of course it was about the administration. But I was tired of living in prison. I gave them twelve years of my life. That was enough."

BIBLIOGRAPHY

"10 Things You Need to Know About Brutality and Abuse at Clinton Correctional Facility," Correctional Association of New York, last modified September 04, 2015, http://www.correctionalassociation.org/news/10-things-you-need-to-know-about-brutality-and-abuse-at-clinton-c-f.

"33-3012 Correctional Officers and Jailers," Standard Occupational Classification, United States Department of Labor, last modified March 11, 2010, https://www.bls.gov/soc/2010/soc333012.htm.

Associated Press, "Sweat: 'I Deeply Apologize,'" Times Union, Feb. 03, 2016, http://www.timesunion.com/local/article/David-Sweat-to-be-sentenced-for-Dannemora-escape-6803242.php.

"Clinton," History of Clinton CF – NYS' Largest & 3d Oldest Prison, New York Correction History Society. Accessed May 2017. http://www.correctionhistory.org/index.html.

Clukey, Keshia, "Personnel changes continue more than a year after Dannemora prison break," PoliticoNew York, Politico, September 02, 2016, https://www.

politico.com/states/new-york/albany/story/2016/09/
reassignments-resignations-continue-more-than-a-year-af-
ter-dannemora-prison-break-105150.

"Conference Call Update on Escaped Inmates with Governor
Cuomo and NYS Public Safety Officials," Governor
Andrew M. Cuomo, SoundCloud, call recorded June
07, 2015, https://soundcloud.com/nygovcuomo/
conference-call-update-on-escaped-inmates-with-governor-
cuomo-and-nys-public-safety-officials.

Cuomo, Andrew, Twitter Post, June 7, 2015,
11:45 AM, https://twitter.com/nygovcuomo/
status/607619420744249344.

"Crime Laboratory System," New York State Police, New York
State, https://troopers.ny.gov/Crime_Laboratory_System/.

"Criminal Justice Statistics," New York State Division of
Criminal Justice Services. Accessed May 2017. http://www.
criminaljustice.ny.gov/crimnet/ojsa/stats.htm.

"Department of Corrections and Community Supervision."
NYS Department of Corrections and Community
Supervision. Accessed March 2016. http://www.doccs.
ny.gov/.

"For Information Directly Leading To The Apprehension
And Arrest, Of Inmates Richard Matt And David Sweat,
Governor Andrew M. Cuomo Is Offering A Reward To
Anyone Who, and Provides Information That Directly
Leads To The Apprehension. R E W A R D." 07 June
2015. Accessed October 2016. https://www.governor.
ny.gov/news/governor-cuomo-announces-100000-re-
ward-information-leading-arrest-escaped-inmates.

"Fugitive Investigations – 15 Most Wanted," U.S. Marshals
Service, June 2015, https://www.usmarshals.gov/investiga-
tions/most_wanted/matt-sweat/photos.htm.

"FULL EPISODE: The Accomplice," NBCNews.com, Sept.
18, 2015, https://www.nbcnews.com/dateline/video/
full-episode--the-accomplice-531519555753.

"Governor Cuomo Provides Update at Clinton Correctional Facility in Dannemora," Flickr, June 06, 2015, https://www.flickr.com/photos/governorandrewcuomo/sets/72157654070293876/.

"Governor Cuomo Announces $100,000 Reward for Information Leading to Arrest of Escaped Inmates," Governor Andrew M. Cuomo, New York State, June 16, 2015, https://www.governor.ny.gov/news/governor-cuomo-announces-100000-reward-information-leading-arrest-escaped-inmates.

Just Us. Facebook. Accessed March 2016. https://www.facebook.com/Just-Us-327631947281371/.

Kim, Eun Kyung. "Gov. Cuomo on Escaped Murderers: 'They Definitely Had Help,'" News, TODAY, June 08, 2015, https://www.today.com/news/gov-cuomo-escaped-murderers-they-definitely-had-help-t24956.

Leahy Scott, Catherine. "Investigation of the June 5, 2015 Escape of Inmates David Sweat and Richard Matt from Clinton Correctional Facility," Albany, NY: State of New York, Office of the Inspector General, 2016. Accessed June 2016. https://ig.ny.gov/sites/default/files/pdfs/DOCCS%20Clinton%20Report%20FINAL_1.pdf.

Mann, Brian, "How Prisons Became the North Country's Normal," Regional News, NCPR, December 2, 2013, https://www.northcountrypublicradio.org/news/story/23381/20131202/how-prisons-became-the-north-country-s-normal.

Mann, Brian, "Listen: Brian Mann Interviewed CO Gene Palmer in 2000 about life inside Dannemora," Regional News, NCPR, June 25, 2015, https://www.northcountrypublicradio.org/news/story/28775/listen-brian-mann-interviewed-co-gene-palmer-in-2000-about-life-inside-dannemora.

mikeraab2, "Church of the Good Thief (9 Minutes),"

video, 8:48, May 03, 2009, https://www.youtube.com/watch?v=WVuftGUjRBE.

"NEW YORK – Clinton County," State Listings, National Register of Historical Places, accessed May 04, 2017, http://www.nationalregisterofhistoricplaces.com/ny/clinton/state.html.

New York Daily News, "Cuomo Tours Maximum-security Prison Where Two Escaped," video, 2:57, June 06, 2015, https://www.youtube.com/watch?v=mpXoSI2mG8E.

"Occupational Employment Statistics," United States Department of Labor, accessed May 04, 2017, https://www.bls.gov/oes/.

Press & Sun Bulletin, "The Tarsia Files: The Hidden Story," Pressconnects., June 10, 2015, http://www.press-connects.com/story/news/public-safety/2015/06/10/tarsia-files-david-sweat/28735471/.

Psychediva, "The Alcatraz Dummies," 6:17, August 17, 2008, https://www.youtube.com/watch?v=t3ZYWKj8g2o.

Schwirtz, Michael, and Winerip, Michael, "An Inmate Dies, and No One Is Punished," The New York Times, December 13, 2015, https://www.nytimes.com/2015/12/14/nyregion/clinton-correctional-facility-in-mate-brutality.html.

Schwirtz, Michael, and Winerip, Michael, "After 2 Killers Fled, New York Prisoners Say, Beatings Were Next," The New York Times, August 11, 2015, https://www.nytimes.com/2015/08/12/nyregion/after-2-killers-fled-new-york-prisoners-say-beatings-were-next.html.

"Significant Industries: A Report to the Workforce Development System," Bureau of Labor Market Information Division of Research and Statistics, New York, Economic and Political Weekly 22.41 (1987): 1720. 2015. Accessed May 2017. https://labor.ny.gov/stats/PDFs/Significant-Industries-North-Country.pdf.

"The Clinton Correctional Facility Report," Correctional

Association of New York, October 19, 2014,
http://www.correctionalassociation.org/news/
the-clinton-correctional-facility-report.

"Video & Photos of Governor Cuomo's Tour of Prison Escape
Route in Dannemora," Governor Andrew M. Cuomo,
New York State, July 13, 2015, https://www.governor.
ny.gov/news/video-photos-governor-cuomos-tour-prison-
escape-route-dannemora.

"Video & Transcript: Governor Cuomo Announces End to
Search for Escaped Inmates Richard Matt and David
Sweat," Governor Andrew M. Cuomo, New York State,
June 28, 2015, https://www.governor.ny.gov/news/
video-transcript-governor-cuomo-announces-end-search-
escaped-inmates-richard-matt-and-david.

"Video Emerges from NY Prison Escapee Richard Matt's Past,"
ABC News, June 23, 2015, http://abcnews.go.com/GMA/
video/video-emerges-ny-prison-escapee-richard-matts-
past-31961055.

Village of Dannemora. Accessed 04 May 2017. https://www.
villageofdannemora.com/.

WPTZ NewsChannel 5, "Governor Holds News Conference
on Prison Escape," YouTube, June 06, 2015, https://www.
youtube.com/watch?v=si5xn55zquU.

WPTZ NewsChannel 5, "Gov. Cuomo: 'Don't Know If They're
in the Immediate Area or in Mexico,'" video, 2:24, https://
www.youtube.com/watch?v=cF9_OE5JZqA.

ACKNOWLEDGMENTS

This book first came about because my agent and now friend, Sharlene Martin of Martin Literary Management, believed in this project. I was thrilled when Sharlene first took me on as a client, and quickly saw why she is the top true crime agent in the business. She has guided me through each phase of the publishing process, and her extensive knowledge of this complicated and competitive market landed us my first book deal. I cannot thank her enough for her commitment to this endeavor, her advocacy for my work, and her steadfast belief in my ability to succeed.

Another huge thanks to Diversion Books. Publisher Jamie Levine and acquisitions editor Lia Ottaviano worked tirelessly behind the scenes to bring this piece to life. Lia went above and beyond with extensive editorial feedback that pushed me to write with greater detail and clarity. I am forever grateful for the time and energy she put into making this story sing.

I could not be more thankful to Ellen Tumposky, one of the smartest editors I know and the person I trusted most to see the first draft of this manuscript. Ellen's feedback—and flexibility, as she somehow squeezed in reading this piece while balancing all her other work—was invaluable. Apart from Sharlene and MLM Editorial Director Anthony Flacco (who also helped shape the direction of this piece), writers Nate Schweber, Khristina Narizhnaya, and Michael Orbach were the first three people to read parts of this work in its infant stage. Their encouragement, praise, and critique only made me better.

I am also indebted to Robert Moore, who has supported my career in journalism since he hired me for a staff position at the *New York Daily News*. Rob, who is head of news at the paper, granted me a six-week sabbatical in October 2016 so that I could work in the Adirondacks. Rob also assigned me to cover the escape when the story first broke. Without that task, I might never have thought to write a book.

To my colleagues at the *News* and other New York media outlets—Edgar Sandoval, Molly Crane-Newman, Barry Paddock, Lorena Mongelli, Jenn Bain, Brigitte Stelzer, Erin Calabrese, Kevin Fasick, Christina Carrega, Priscilla DeGregory, Arielle Dollinger, Seth J. Bookey, C.J. Sullivan, Michael Schwartz, David Wexler, Dennis Clark, Ginger Adams Otis, Kevin Sheehan, Todd Maisel, Yana Paskova, Peggy Ackermann, Marcus Santos, Anthony DelMundo, Debbie Egan-Chin, Laura Dimon, James Keivom, Reggie Lewis, Craig Ruttle, Lisa Colangelo, Larry McShane, Peter Gerber, Ken Garger, Trevor Kapp, Michael

Daly, Ken Murray, Sam Costanza, Johnny Rocca, and many others—you are the reason I love this business.

I've been blessed to have several mentors in life. Yvonne Latty and Julia Lieblich, my former professors and now dear friends from New York University and Loyola University Chicago, respectively, were among the very first to encourage me to pursue this line of work. I can only hope to emulate their strong sense of compassion, high ethical standards, and commitment to this craft. Joanne Gerr, who at times knows me better than I know myself, has guided me through every one of life's trials in the last seven years. I do not know where I would be without her.

I am also nothing without my parents. My mom, Michele, and dad, Joseph, believed in me when I did not believe in myself. They continually strive to be a better version of themselves—a quality I am so grateful that they instilled in me. Their love knows no bounds, and neither does my love for them.

My family—my aunts Joanne Marcius and Elaine Marcius, brother Blake Petrenchik, and those who have passed on, my beloved uncle Tom Marcius and grandfather Michael Taddeo—is the best anyone could ever ask for. My grandmothers, Rose Taddeo and Elizabeth (Yenchick) Marcius, passed away during the final phases of editing the manuscript. Rose saw the cover of this book ten days before she died, and expressed great joy in knowing that I would be a published author. Elizabeth, a woman who underestimated her own gift for the written word, also lived long enough to know that this project would come to fruition. She had one dying wish for me, her only grandchild: that I continue to write. This work is dedicated to them.

Strong friendships got me through. Regina Kenney, Noura Khoury, and Julie Maskulka live hundreds of miles away from New York, and yet always found time to reach out and ask how I was holding up. Jocelyn Tice and Melyssa Hurley have been my lifeline, often taking the time out of their busy schedules to grab drinks and discuss every up and down of this process. I could not be more blessed to also have Zoe Borenstein and Juan Gamboa, some of my dearest friends in the city, who have been with me from the beginning. Then there is Ryan Chavis, Kathryn Kattalia, Sierra McCleary-Harris, Emily Canal, Amanda Plasencia DiLillo, and Meredith Bennett-Smith, who have been there for me since our first days of grad school. Frank Rosario took every late-night phone call when I wondered how I was going to pull this off, and even stepped up to help transcribe a very long interview when I was up against another deadline. Mark Morales—a reporter for *New York Newsday* whose passion for journalism is only surpassed by the qualities he brings to the table as a friend—talked me through every hurdle that came my way. Lucille Burrascano, one of the first female detectives to join the ranks of New York's Finest, brainstormed with me when I began to delve into narrative. A special thanks to Danny Angen, whose support early on in this endeavor meant more to me than he knows. I'm also forever grateful for the companionship of my pets, especially my beloved dog Otto, an animal with boundless intelligence, intuition, and spirit. He accompanied me on every single trip to the Adirondacks, and often sat at my feet while I wrote.

The people I interviewed made this book possible. David Sweat had no incentive to talk (monetary or otherwise) and yet he agreed to speak with me. Sgt. Jay Cook went above and beyond. He invited me into the Malone Barracks, introduced me to his colleagues, and spent a great deal of time examining every day of the manhunt to make sure law enforcement's perspective was accurately represented. Corrections Officer John Stockwell took me into his home and shared every detail of the day that changed the course of the manhunt. Michael and Terry Ann McCaffrey—who live in the North Country and who I first met the day Richard Matt was shot—have been with me through it all. (Terry put me up for a week while I reported upstate. Michael introduced me to people he knew had their own stories. He even helped me map out Matt and Sweat's entire route through the mountains. I am forever in their debt.) There are also those COs and state contractors I spoke with but have not named at their request. Their information was instrumental in constructing this narrative.

There is no greater privilege than people trusting you to tell their story. I only hope they feel I have done it justice.

CHELSIA ROSE MARCIUS is a staff reporter at the *New York Daily News* covering crime, courts, politics, and breaking news. She has been interviewed a number of times on radio and television—including *MSNBC, BBC Radio, Fox 5 New York,* and *Inside Edition*—to discuss her work. Ms. Marcius has broken exclusive stories while covering some of the biggest national news events of the past five years, such as the Boston Marathon bombing, the abduction of three women held captive for years in Cleveland, and the mass shootings at Mandalay Bay in Las Vegas, Pulse nightclub in Orlando, and Sandy Hook Elementary School in Newtown, Connecticut.

In New York City, Ms. Marcius and *Daily News* photographer Ken Murry were the first to interview Ramsey Orta, the man who filmed the death of Eric Garner in 2014. Her reporting on this event helped the paper win the *Associated Press* award for continuing coverage. She was also part of a team of *Daily News* journalists who took home a *Deadline Club* Award for their coverage of the Second Avenue subway explosion in 2015.

Ms. Marcius is an adjunct journalism professor at New York University. She lives on the Upper East Side in Manhattan with her beloved pets, Miss Olivia, Mo, and Otto.